Verse-by-verse through *HEBREWS:*
A Study Guide, Vol. I

By Ron Merryman

Published by:
MERRYMAN MINISTRIES
Colorado Springs, CO 80918

ISBN 978-0-9700994-9-5

Other publications by the author:

Books:

Galatians: God's Antidote to Legalism, a verse-by-verse commentary

Justification by Faith Alone & Its Historical Challenges

Analytical Notes on Daniel, an analysis of every paragraph of *Daniel* with an emphasis on the prophetical sections

Growth Truth for Believers (a series of booklets):

The Text of Scripture: Which Text? A Case for Moderation in the King James Only Debate

The Amazing Ministries of the Holy Spirit: Resource for Every Believer

Understanding James 2:14-26: Removing the Theological Tension Between Faith & Good Works

The Passion War: Spiritual conflict in Every Believer

The Believer & The Mosaic Law: How doe these Relate?

Spirituality...Maturation...Retrogression

Additional copies of this book can be ordered from:

Merryman Ministries
5531 Spoked Wheel Drive
Colorado Springs, CO 80918
Email: rcmerryman@earthlink.net

TABLE OF CONTENTS

Dedication

Not only do Ben, my son, and Sandra, my wife, provide daily encouragement in the things of the Lord, they also provided the voluntary labor to get this text to the printer. Happily and affectionately, I dedicate it to them.

PLEASE READ BEFORE PROCEEDING

This book is written for serious students of the Biblical text, both the English and the Greek texts. Balancing the information of/from both texts is like walking a tightrope, difficult to say the least. The issue: how does one draw <u>every</u> serious student of God's Word into the text and its meaning?

<u>For students of the English text</u>: the expository outlines and comments, the contextual reviews, the thought-flow summaries, even the comments on word usage should help fulfill this purpose.

<u>For students of the Greek text</u>: I have supplied a Greek Ready Reference section (Addendum A) on verbs, verbals, and conditional sentences. In the verse-by-verse comments, locations of many of these are marked with an asterisk (*), which refers the reader to the Ready References. I very much want to encourage pastors and teachers to make good exegetical use of their study of Koine Greek.

Efforts to balance the information herein so that it helps both types of students is illustrated in my explanation of Hebrews 6:4-8 where the Greek grammar is explained with the student of the English text in mind. Many of you know that that paragraph has suffered innumerable interpretations and abuse over the centuries.

Regardless of your affinities in textual studies, I trust this book will help you understand the glorious truths of Jesus Christ, the Messiah, presented in the *Epistle to the Hebrews*. May this study contribute to the glorification that He alone deserves.

-Ron Merryman
Colorado Springs, CO
August, 2005

INTRODUCTION: The Book of Hebrews

<u>a. the readers</u>
<u>b. the problem</u>
<u>c. the nature of the letter</u>
<u>d. the writer</u>
<u>e. the date</u>
<u>f. an outline</u>

The Book of Hebrews is the Holy Spirit's commentary on the Mosaic Economy, Jewish life under the Sinaitic or Levitical Covenant, contrasted with salvation provided by Christ, the Messiah. The details of that economy were so familiar to the readers that Old Testament passages are quoted without stating specific references. The writer assumes such references unnecessary: his readers knew well the Old Testament.

The Readers

To whom was this marvelous letter addressed: Believers or Unbelievers? Or, as per some commentators, "ones who had stopped short of real faith in Jesus Christ;" that is, "almost believers?" Or to a mixture, some believers and some "almost believers?" Let the text decide: note how the author addresses his readers (*New King James Version*: as are all scripture quotes herein unless otherwise specified):

3:1   *Therefore, <u>holy brethren</u>, <u>partakers of the heavenly calling</u>...*

4:16   *Let <u>us</u> therefore come boldly to the throne of grace, that <u>we</u> may obtain mercy and find grace to help in time of need.*

5:12   *For though by this time <u>you ought to be teachers</u>...*

6:9   *But, <u>beloved</u>, we are confident of better things <u>concerning you</u>, yes, <u>things that accompany salvation</u>, though we speak in this manner.*

10:24-26 *And <u>let us consider one another</u> in order to stir up love and good works, not forsaking the assembling of ourselves together...*

10:39 *<u>But we are not of those who draw back to perdition, but of those who believe to the saving of the soul</u>.*

12:28 *Therefore, since <u>we are receiving</u> a kingdom which cannot be shaken, <u>let us have grace by which we may serve God acceptably</u> with reverence and godly fear.*

13:20-21 *Now may the God of peace who brought up our Lord Jesus from the dead, that great Shepherd of the sheep, through the blood of the everlasting covenant, 21 <u>make you complete in every good work</u> to do His will, <u>working</u>*

This and all corresponding pages left blank for the reader's personal notes.

> *in you what is well pleasing in His sight, through Jesus Christ, to whom be glory forever and ever. Amen.*
>
> **13:22** *And I appeal to you, brethren, bear with the word of exhortation, for I have written to you in few words.*

Such terms of address and statements <u>could not</u> have been written to unbelievers. The evidence is overwhelming: we must conclude that the readers were believers.

The warnings, however, lead most commentators to conclude (incorrectly) that some had stopped short of salvation, hence were almost saved, not true believers. A number of these writers state that the book in general is to believers, but the warnings to unbelievers (particularly those in 5:11-6:12 and in 10:19-39). I have eleven commentaries on *Hebrews*: every one of which holds this view. Though reluctant to buck such collective wisdom, my study of the text proves otherwise. All the warnings are for believers.

Logically, <u>all</u> Scripture is for the Believer: it serves as a basis for doctrine, conviction, correction and instruction (2Tim. 3:16). Moreover, why write scripture to an unbeliever? Scripture is written <u>about</u> unbelievers, but not <u>to</u> unbelievers.

The Problem

But though believers, they were somewhat unique. First of all, they were Hebrew Christians, Jews who owned Jesus as Savior and Messiah. Secondly: they were undergoing severe persecution from their families and fellow countryman because of their faith. Thirdly, and most importantly: they were being tempted to return to the ongoing ritual of the Jewish Temple and the confused doctrines of first century Judaism. Even Peter and the Eleven had problems sorting out the confusion of that outmoded system. Sacrificial offerings for sin ceased in AD 70 with the destruction of the Temple in Jerusalem. Hence <u>the temptation to return to Temple sacrifices was unique to this generation of Jewish believers, a fact critical to one's interpretation and application of this book.</u>

The confusion and ambiguity of believing in Christ's (Messiah's) death as God's final and only answer to sin, then returning to the Temple to make sacrifices for sin is apparent. But such acts would be worse than confusing: they would undermine the work of the Cross and make the blood/death of Christ appear ineffectual.

The Nature of the Letter

Thus, the writer addresses himself to the Glories of Christ, His superiority over anything that existed in the Mosaic-Levitical Economy, and the absolute value and finality of His death. Christ is seen as the Son of God (1:5,8), the Son of Man (2:5-3:6), the perfect High Priest (4:14-9:24), the one and only efficacious Sacrifice for sins (10:1-12), and the living Way to God (10:19-13:25). He boldly states twice on Chapter 10: "*...there remains no more sacrifice for sins*" (10:18 & 26).

Interspersed among these doctrinal truths are a series of warning-type admonitions that in

almost every case revolve around the issue of moving on both in <u>the faith</u>, the body of Christian truth, and in personal <u>faith</u>, the application of Christian truth to daily living. Faith in *Hebrews* as elsewhere in the New Testament is always actively motivated by the quality of its object (God, Christ, or His Word). Christian faith is a living response, never to be stagnant.

The Writer

The writer has been identified variously: many say Paul, some say Apollos, Barnabas, Luke, plus others. The early church confessed to uncertainty in this regard. Paul could not have written the letter because:

1) The author of Hebrews places himself in the second generation of believers, one who received the Gospel second hand (2:3). Paul categorically denies second hand reception of the Gospel (Gal. 1:11ff.).

2) The literary style (Greek text) is not that of Paul. Contrasting Paul's style with the writer of *Hebrews*:

   -the language is not that of Paul;
   -the method is not that of Paul;
   -the technique of quoting the Old Testament is not that of Paul;
   -the smooth rhetorical style of Hebrews is not that of Paul;
   -the writer uses the LXX differently than does Paul.

3) Paul claims to always attach his name to his letters, often in his own hand (Gal. 6:1, Col. 4:18, 1Cor. 16:21, 2Thess. 3:17). The writer of Hebrews omits his name.

4) Paul's primary ministry was to Gentiles, not Jews (Gal. 2:8).

5) The mention of Timothy's release from prison (13:23) and the Author's own imprisonment (10:34) do not necessitate our viewing Paul as the author.

Who wrote the Book of Hebrews? We do not know, but Barnabas, Apollos, and even Luke qualify.

The Date

Hebrews had to be written while sacrifices were yet being offered in the Temple in Jerusalem. Present tense verbs and verbals are used regarding Temple sacrificial ritual in 8:4-5; 10:11; and 13:10. Obviously, the Temple, which was destroyed by the Romans in AD 70, was still standing when this epistle was penned. Hebrews was written shortly before that date, probably around 68AD.

An Outline of Hebrews

Two chief topics comprise this letter:

      I. THE GLORIES OF MESSIAH, THE CHRIST, Ch. 1-10

     II. THE APPLICATION TO CHRISTIANS, Ch. 11-13

Interspersed in the text are a series of five practical admonitions and warnings characterized by an appeal to active faith (the hortatory, *"Let us ..."*).

I. The Glories of Messiah, the Christ, Ch. 1-10

Key Idea: CHRIST is SUPERIOR to all messengers and aspects of the Old Covenant

A. 1:1-3 to Prophets

B. 1:4-2:18 to Angels

    (2:1-4, 1st series of admonitions/warnings)

C. 3:1-6 to Moses

    (3:7-4:7, 2nd series of admonitions/warnings)

D. 4:8-10 to Joshua

    (4:11-13, 2nd series of admonitions/warnings continued)

E. 4:14-10:18 to any High Priest and their sacrifices

    (5:11-6:12, 3rd series of admonitions/warnings)

    (10:19-39, 4th series of admonitions/warnings)

II. The Application to Christians, Ch. 11-13

A. 11:1-40 Active Faith Illustrated

B. 12:1-2 Active Faith Encouraged

    (12:1-13:25, 5th series of admonitions/warnings)

INTRODUCTORY SUMMARY

Hebrews is an Epistle written to first century Christians who had Jewish backgrounds and were being tempted to return to the religion and forms of Temple worship. To do so would be a disgrace to the person and work of Messiah. So in effect the Book is saying:

Chapter 1	Do not deny the Deity of Christ
Chapter 2	Do not drift from Salvation in Christ
Chapter 3-4	Do not doubt the promises of God
Chapter 5-6	Do not degenerate or retrogress in the Christian life
Chapter 7-10	Do not downgrade or undermine Christ's Priesthood and Sacrifice
Chapter 11	Do not despair: take hope thru examples of faith
Chapter 12-13	Do not depart from the way of Christ

Hebrews 1:1-3

The first chapter of <u>Hebrews</u> is in a larger context (Chapters 1-3) that compares Christ with the messengers of the Old Covenant, the prophets, angels, and Moses. The Deity of Christ is immediately and clearly revealed (v. 2-12). As all light sources pale in comparison to those of the sun, so all preliminary and preceding information about God in comparison with that of His Son, the Lord Jesus Christ. The essence of the Son and His sacrificial work will form the basis for the New Covenant and the inherent excellences of Christianity. The Son Himself is God's final message to mankind. Knowing the readers were tempted to revert to the religious forms of Judaism, it is little wonder that the Author plunges immediately into the glorious essence of Christ.

Verses 1-3 compare God's communication in His Son to that of the Old Testament prophets. Verses 4-14 compare Him to angels. This chapter contains some of the clearest and most pointed statements on the Deity of Christ in all of the New Testament.

I. CHRIST, THE FINALITY OF GOD'S REVELATION, 1:1-3

The major emphasis of these introductory verses is that the Son (of God) brings to mankind a far greater revelation of God than could have been brought through the prophets: the quality of that revelation is perfect, the nature of it final and complete.

A. God's Old Testament revelation, v. 1, Prophet Mediators.

1:1 *God, who at various times and in various ways spoke in time past to the fathers by the prophets,*

1. How the Old Testament came

- **"in many portions, parts"**: the idea is in separate revelations ("various times" is a little misleading): numerous separate revelations from God were necessary to complete the O.T. canon. It did not come all at once in one package.

- **"in various or many ways"**: these revelations from God came in diverse ways: dreams, visions, theophanies, through types, through angels, etc. The author is interested in contrasting this with the finality and completeness of what God has to say in His Son.

2. By whom it came

- **"by (in) the prophets"**: includes Moses, David, Daniel, and the writers of the Old Testament. Some of these functioned as prophets, but in real life did not have the office of prophet (both David and Daniel were involved in Royal courts: but they were also prophets). God, in the Old Testament times, chose to reveal His plan through a variety of prophets over a long period of time.

3. To whom it came

   -**"to the fathers"**: the various Old Testament revelations were directed to the Patriarchs and authoritative leaders of Israel.

B. God's New Testament Revelation, vs. 2-3. The Son as Mediator .

1:2-3 *...has in these last days spoken to us by His Son, whom He has appointed heir of all things, through whom also He made the worlds; 3 who being the brightness of His glory and the express image of His person, and upholding all things by the word of His power, when He had by Himself purged our sins, sat down at the right hand of the Majesty on high...*

God Who spoke in Old Testament times by prophets "in the last of these days (last of O.T. times) has spoken (aorist tense*) unto us in a Son." A dramatic contrast with v. 1 is intended. God spoke in the end of Old Testament days in or by one who stands in relationship to Him as a Son: the stress is upon the uniqueness of the Divine-Son-type communication contrasted with that of prophets. Involved is the birth of Messiah, His essential nature and all that He accomplished both as the Son of God and as the Word of God. In the O.T., the prophets were God's messengers, now God's actual Son becomes the herald. He Himself is the final message of God to mankind.

Note the sevenfold witness concerning His Son: these facts bring out His greatness and show why the revelation in Him is final and complete:

1. He is appointed heir of all, v. 2: Every existing thing in the universe is to be possessed by the Son. He is the heir of the cosmos: in view particularly is the world to come (compare v. 6 & 2:5). This heirship is based upon the Son taking upon Himself the form of a man and volitionally suffering the death of the cross. Now exalted at the right hand of God, He is destined to inherit all things, and these He will share with believers, who themselves are joint heirs with Him (Gal. 3:26; 4:6,7; Rom. 8 : 17).

2. He is the executor of the time-space-creation v. 2: "By whom he made the *worlds*" (lit. "ages:" αιων / *aion*: the word relates to categories or periods of history from Divine viewpoint such as the Antediluvian Age, the Postdiluvian Age, the Jewish Age, the Church Age, the Millennial Age). This means that the Son was God's intermediary who both made (the verb is aorist tense from ποιεω / *poieo*, "to make a product) and arranged all things in the time-space-universe, mapping out God's plan for each age. The One who made the ages is certainly far superior to anyone who prophesies within an age! Col. 1:16, *"by Him were all things created,"* and John 1:3, *"all things were made by Him,"* reaffirm the fact that the pre-incarnate Christ as the Son was the creator of the universe and its time-space-categories.

3. He is the radiation of God's Glory, v.3. Jesus Christ in the days of His flesh is the perfect expression of the very essence of God. "Brightness" and "radiance" (NASV) translates απαυγασμα / *apaugasma*, "light radiation," "effulgence,"

"out-raying," "radiant splendor." Its rays tell the glory and brilliance of the sun. In like manner, the glory of the Father God shines through the Son (in the person of Messiah) to the human race.

The dilemma: John 1:18, "No man has seen at any time" (so as to be able to tell forth His glories); God's solution: "the only begotten Son ("only begotten God", critical texts, NASV), which is in the bosom of the Father, that one has exegeted or fully explained Him," John 1:18. See also John 14: 9 where Jesus says, "He that has seen me has seen the Father." Jesus Christ, has fully told or manifested God because He is the radiance or out-raying of God's glorious essence. Anyone who wants to know God must look at Jesus Christ. One should not fail to note that we are not yet through the first sentence of the letter and already the glories of the Son who took on human form are being told!

4. He is the exact representation of God's essence, v. 3. "Express image" and "representation" are translations of χαρακτηρ / *charaktēr* (found only here in the N.T.).   Christ the Son is the exact character of God's substance or essence (υποστασις / *hupostasis*). Stated another way: God's essential essence is made manifest in the Son who became flesh and dwelt among us. Just as an image on a coin corresponds to that on the die, so the Son of God manifests the image of the Father.

5. He bears or sustains all things by His Omnipotent Word , v. 3. Christ not only made the Ages, His Word upholds their courses.   Creative utterance requires sustaining utterance: He provides both. Physical laws are His laws: they operate by His decree; consequently, the laws of nature or scientific law rightly understood relate to the decree or word of the Son of God. (See Psalm 33:9; Heb. 11:3; Col. 3:16,17).

To this point, these statements (#1-5) relate the essence of the Son to the cosmos. #6 will focus on His personal relation with man and man's sin;   #7 with His exaltation as a man over men, angels and the universe.

6. He Himself made purification for sins, v.3. The verbal (participle) "made" is middle voice (ποιησαμενος / *poiēsamenos*) indicating the Son's intense interest in His redemptive act and the results thereof. The tense is aorist, meaning the job is done, complete, finished. It never needs repetition! "Purification" (καθαρισμος / *katharismos*) means cleansing from sin's guilt, corruption and uncleanness.

The point is that the Son by becoming flesh and dying for the sins of mankind has made all the cleansing necessary for sin from God's point of view. There is, in fact, no other cleansing available: even the blood of bulls and goats under the old economy could not take away sin, Heb. 10:4.

To this point, the name Jesus Christ has not even been used; the readers knew that these statements relating to the Son could only be understood as fulfilled in the humanity of the Messiah, the Lord Jesus Christ.

7. <u>He sat down at God's right hand</u> (after making cleansing for our sins) v. 3. This signifies the finality and completeness of the sacrificial work of Christ. His perfect sacrifice is ratified or guaranteed by His resurrection (Rom. 1:4): His exaltation is begun in the ascension: His worthiness, royal dignity and majesty are recognized by His seating in session at God's right hand until all His enemies are made His footstool (comp.v.13). His seating is indicative of a job completed. The right hand of God is the place of victory, prestige, power, authority, and supremacy for the man Christ Jesus.

<u>Precious is the thought that every Believer is seated there with Him due to the identity/position they have in Christ, Eph. 2:5,6.</u>

The writer of Hebrews wastes no time getting his readers into the excellencies of God's communication in His Son. The rest of Chapter One concerns itself with a contrast between Christ and angels. Again, the Deity of the Son is clearly stated along with statements that could only apply to his humanity.

Hebrews 1:4-14

II. CHRIST'S INFINITE WORTHINESS AS THE SON OF GOD: ANGELIC INFERIORITY, 1:4-14

1:3 ends with the Son as Messiah sitting in His humanity at the right hand of God: 1:4 begins, ***"having become so much better than angels..."***

This phrase introduces the superiority of Jesus Christ over angels. The emphasis <u>is not</u> on His eternal Son-ship of the past, but on His <u>exaltation</u> as a <u>human being</u> (post resurrection, of course). There is a MAN in heaven; He is the Son of God and God the Son, but nevertheless a MAN, the Son as the Messiah. 1:4-14 will develop the contrast between His transcendent majesty and the lesser qualities of the angelic host (the word "angels" occurs eleven times in the first two chapters). Nowhere in the New Testament is the Deity of Christ stated more clearly.

A. The superiority of His name, v.4.

> ***1:4 having become so much better than the angels, as He has by inheritance obtained a more excellent name than they.***

<u>My Translation:</u> *"Because having become* (or "because being made": the participle, aorist tense of γινομαι/*ginomai*, is adverbial of cause*) *so much better than angels, He has inherited* (perfect tense* of κληροω / *kleroō*, indicating the permanence of the inheritance) *a far superior name than them. "*

Christ's full name and its significance is indicative of the intrinsic value of His person from God's point of view. His full title in exaltation is the Lord Jesus Christ, the Son of God.

1. The name

    "Lord" - <u>authority</u> emphasis: He is sovereign both in heaven and earth (compare Mt. 28:18, where Christ states it Himself).

    "Jesus" - <u>savior</u> emphasis: note that this is the name closely related to His humanity. The name is a contraction of the Hebrew *Jehoshua* which means "Jehovah saves" or "will help", or "savior".

    "Christ" - <u>Messiah</u> emphasis: "the Anointed One", God's Son, promised in the Old Testament: Deity is involved in this name (Psa. 2 & 110).

    "Son of God" - <u>Deity</u> emphasis: relates to eternal relationship in the Godhead

2. The "better" name

In His humanity, Jesus Christ, the Messiah, is Lord: as such, He is superior in position and authority than the highest of the angelic sphere. Contrasted is the "betterness" of His humanity to angelic beings (as illustrated below).

Figure #1 Christ as a MAN exalted higher than ANGELS

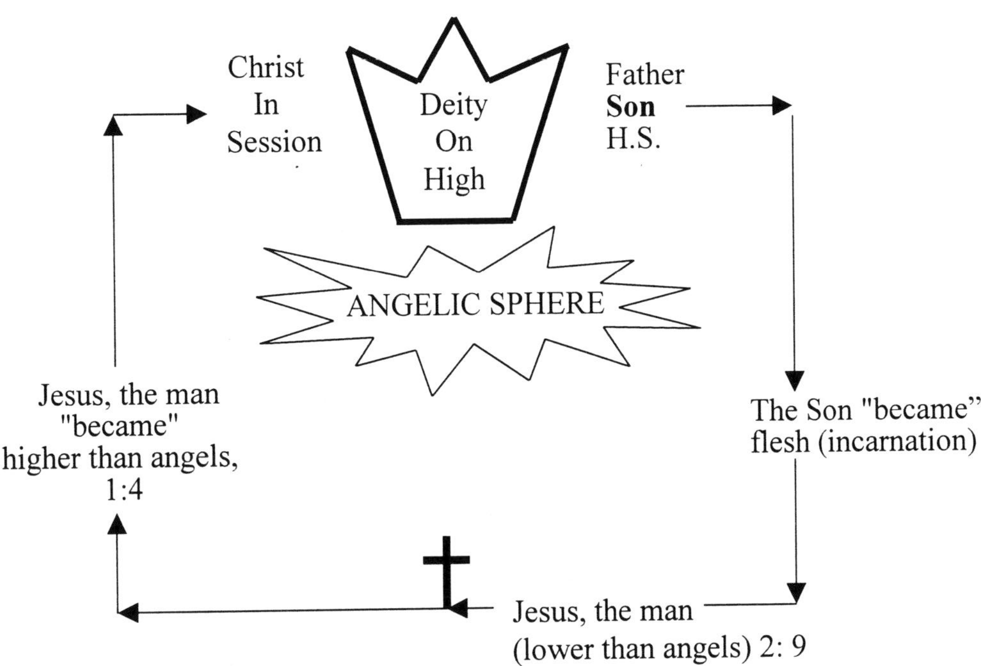

That Christ in His humanity is far superior to angels is stated as fact in verses 3b and 4 : verses 5 - 14 support the fact. What is the author's point? Why this focus? The following facts help us understand the issues:

a. Angels were involved in revealing parts of the Law to Moses (Gal. 3:19; Heb. 2:2; Acts 7:53); but the Judaism of Jesus' day held that the entire Law was given by disposition of angels. The writer is correcting this undue exaltation of angels.

b. Though angels have their place in God's economy, they cannot compare with God speaking in His incarnate Son. This is the message of Hebrews 1.

c. Moreover, Christ now sits in session in His incarnate state far above all angelic beings (Heb. 1:3, 13). His exaltation is presented in chapter one: the necessity for His humanity will be presented in Chapter Two.

d. It is important for us to know that angels were created with various capacities and intelligences to fulfill Divine design. Angels are organized and ranked: there is order in the angelic sphere. And, though angels are of a higher order than mankind (Psalm. 8:4-6; Heb. 2:6-9), Christ as a man is now

exalted far above the angelic host because of the victory of His Cross. Moreover, every believer is seated in Christ in the heavenlies far above all principalities and powers (angels). We share His exalted state, Eph. 1:20; 2:5,6.

B. The superiority of His relationship with the Father (verses that of angels), v. 5

1:5 *For to which of the angels did He ever say: "You are My Son, Today I have begotten You"? And again: "I will be to Him a Father, And He shall be to Me a Son"?*

V.5 begins a series of rhetorical questions to illustrate the transcendent majesty of Christ. "Did God ever say to any of the angels, 'Thou art my Son, this day have I begotten Thee?'" Answer, "Emphatically, no!" Psalm 2:7 and 2Samuel 7:14 are quoted.

1. Absolute status quo essence: ***"You are my Son."***

In view is the eternal Son who became the Messiah via incarnation (physical birth through the Virgin Mary). Christ stands in relation to the Father as His unique, eternal Son.

2. Incarnation: ***"This day have I begotten Thee."***

Every quote of Psalm 2:7 in the New Testament is a reference to the Incarnation (Acts 13:33; Heb.1:5; 5:5). Christ's birth is in view, not His resurrection nor ascension: Acts 13:33 refers to His being "raised up in   the nation by means of His incarnation" (cmp. Acts 13:22, 23 & 33).

3. Reaffirmation: ***"I will be to Him a father and He shall be to me a Son."***

The quotation is II Sam. 7:14 where God covenants with David concerning David's son who was to reign. Solomon is in view in 2Samuel, but prophetically, Christ alone could fulfill the covenant promises given there (cmp. 2Sam. 7:13-16 and Luke 1:31-33). The point of Hebrews 1:5 is that the son of David, the Lord Jesus Christ, is also the Son of God: Jesus confirms this in Mt. 22:41-46. Angels have never been so addressed by God nor has any enjoyed such a unique relationship with God the Father. The hypostatic union: undiminished Deity in Christ's perfect humanity is the emphasis of this verse.

C. The superiority of His worthiness (angels worship Him), v.6

1:6 *But when He again brings the firstborn into the world, He says: "Let all the angels of God worship Him."*

<u>My Translation</u>: *"And when He brings the first Begotten One again into the inhabited world, He is saying, 'and let all the angels of God worship Him.'"*

1. <u>The time</u>: ***"when He again brings..."*** The reference is to the 2nd Advent. In the 1st Advent, a multitude of angels praise God (Luke 2:13-14), but in the 2nd Advent, <u>all the</u> <u>elect</u> angels will worship Christ just as God is worshipped. Worship is the Messiah's right by virtue of His essence and His work. Angels will worship Him not only as Creator, but as Victor in the great angelic conflict, a victory won at the cross and totally manifested at His 2nd Advent.

2. <u>The object of worship</u>: Christ as ***"the first begotten,"*** *"the pre-eminent one,"* (πρωτοτοκος / *prōtotokos*, meaning first in primacy, the one who has priority, the head of all creation). <u>His position of superiority is in view, not His primogeniture.</u> See Col. 1:15,18; Rev. 1:5; Rom. 8:29 for similar uses of *prōtotokos.*

3. <u>The action</u>: ***"worship Him"***; the verb is aorist imperative of προσκυνεω / *proskuneō*, which see in Mt. 4:10; John 4:23,24; Rev. 11:26, where God the Father is the object of worship. See also Mt. 2:2,11; 9:18; 14:33; 28:17; Mk. 5:6; Lu. 24:52; John 9:38, where Christ is the object of worship. The point is that the Son as the Messiah has the same right to be worshipped as does absolute Deity! And angels will worship Him at the 2nd Advent.

V.5 & 6 say in effect: *"God never addressed any angel as His unique Son: angels do not have such identity, but He did state that angels would worship the Son just as He Himself is worshipped!"*

D. The superiority of His authority (He is sovereign; angels serve), v.7-9

> **1:7-9** ***And of the angels He says: "Who makes His angels spirits And His ministers a flame of fire." 8 But to the Son He says: "Your throne, O God, is forever and ever; A scepter of righteousness is the scepter of Your Kingdom. 9 You have loved righteousness and hated lawlessness; Therefore God, Your God, has anointed You With the oil of gladness more than Your companions."***

V.7 & 8 are a "men-de" (μεν...δε) construction in Greek, which is normally not translated into English: "men-de" constructions normally contrast one thing with another so that the translation could well read:

"<u>ON THE ONE HAND</u> (μεν) relative to angels, He says, 'The One making His angels spirits and His ministers a flame of fire;'

"<u>BUT ON THE OTHER HAND</u> (*de*) relative to the Son, 'Your throne, O God, (is) forever and ever: and the sceptre of uprightness (is) the sceptre of your kingdom.' "

V.7 quotes Psalm 104:4,8; Psalm 45:6,7, both from the LXX.

1. Relative to.(προς / *pros*, lit. *toward*) angels, v.7

God makes angels, who are spirits, serve as His ministers just as lightning or flames of fire serve His purposes. Angels are mighty beings, but still only servants of God and greatly inferior to the Son, both in essence and position in the Divine schemata. The Son on the other hand is referred to as "God".

2. Relative to (προς / *pros* = lit. *"toward"*) the Son, v.8-9

The Father addresses the Son as Deity and this nature of Deity brings everlasting stability and immutability to His throne. Note that the Father does not "make" the Son anything (contrast with angels in v.7), He merely declares what He is, Deity. In v.8, the Son is addressed by the Father as "God", in v.10 as "Lord". No clearer statements of the Deity of Christ are found in the New Testament! The allusion is to the earthly ministry both past and future of Messiah, God's Son.

a. the Son's throne, in perpetuity: it will exist long after the Millennium.

b. the Son's kingdom rule, in righteousness or uprightness. The sceptre or rod of His authority guarantees undeviating justice and the principles of uprightness. Earth's golden age will arrive when mercy and justice are mediated through the Son of God on earth: His nature and character will insure it.

c. the Son's love (v.9), righteousness, the very character of the Son in the days of His flesh as the Lord Jesus Christ: He loved righteousness, what is right from Divine viewpoint. He did no sin (1Pet. 2:22); He knew no sin (2Cor. 5:21); in Him was no sin (1John 3:5).

d. the Son's hatred, lawlessness (ανομια / *anomia*): our Lord hated anything contrary to God's will and rule. Both verbs, loved and hated are in the aorist tense: they sum up, as a ball-of-wax fact, the lifetime mental attitude of Jesus Christ toward God the Father. He loved God's absolute righteousness; He hated disobedience to God's will.

e. the Son's anointing, the joy of kingly office and sovereign authority: the clause could be translated, *"therefore, O God, thy God has anointed You with the oil of joy above They fellows"*. In view is the coronation and consecration of the kingly office (cmp. 1Sam. 10:1,16:13). Christ's anointing is superior in character and consecration and joy to all those who have occupied the throne of David (or any throne for that matter) Psalm 45:6,7 are quoted.

Conclusion: Angels as servants of God do His bidding, but the Son as the Messiah (Deity in flesh) enjoys the position of sovereignty in the universe, a sovereignty that will make itself known upon the earth in a kingdom where righteousness reigns. His second advent will usher in that kingdom.

E. The superiority of His dignity as the Creator, v. 10-12

1:10-12   *And: "You, LORD, in the beginning laid the foundation of the earth, And the heavens are the work of Your hands. 11 They will perish, but You remain; And they will all grow old like a garment; 12 Like a cloak You will fold them up, And they will be changed. But You are the same, And Your years will not fail."*

The Son as Messiah is now addressed as *"Lord"*. These words by the Father declare His creatorship, His immutability, His eternality.   Psalm 102:25-27 is quoted.

1. His creatorship, v.10

- *"**and** you, Lord"*: *"and"* joins two vocatives, that of v.8 and this of v.10, so that the Son is addressed both as *"God"* and *"Lord"* by the Father: an unparalleled emphasis on His Deity! The name in the Psalm (102:26) is actually *Jehovah* (יהוה/ Yhwh)!

- *"**did found on earth**"*: the verb, aorist active of θεμελιοω / *themelioō*, "to found" or "to lay the foundation of something", means that the Son Himself carried out the original acts of creation.

V.9 ended with Messiah reigning as a king: v.10 indicates that He is above and beyond any and all finite beings. He is the unique Creator of the very universe that He enters as the Messiah years after He created it.

2. His immutability, v.11-12

A marked contrast between the creator, who is the Son of God, and His creation is intended in these two verses:

The creation	The Creator, God's eternal Son
- *"**they** shall perish"*: not in the sense of cessation, but of destruction (so as to make way for the new heavens and new earth).	-*"but **you**, **yourself** (in contrast) keep on remaining"*: the verb is an intensified form of μενω / *menō* in the present tense, active voice*.
- *"**they** all will wear out like a garment: **you** will roll them up like a robe: like a garment, **they** will be changed"* (by the new heavens and new earth)	- *"but **you**, **yourself** (in contrast) are* (or "keep on being") *the same: your years will not fail."*

Note that v.10 & 11 take us from His creative acts in the past all the way to His

dealings relative to planet earth in the future. In direct contrast to a universe that is winding down and wearing out like a piece of clothing (the Law of Entropy) is an unchangeable, eternal, immutable Creator. And He is the Son who became the Messiah-man! In v.2, we were told, *"He upholds all things by the word of His power"*: that is, all things are under His control and dependent upon Him. Now we are told that He will one day change the created order to suit His purposes for eternity.

<u>Conclusion:</u> the immutability of the Son, His creative power, His eternal self-existence, clearly demonstrate His Lordship over all created beings. We are not dealing with a simple human being when we deal with the Messiah. His transcendent majesty as God's Son and His message as God's final communication demand that we hear Him: other communicators in the Divine plan such as prophets and angels must be kept in proper perspective.

F. The superiority of His sovereign-session as the Messiah-man: Angelic servitude, v.13,14

    1:13-14 *But to which of the angels has He ever said: "Sit at My right hand, till I make Your enemies Your footstool"? 14 Are they not all ministering spirits sent forth to minister for those who will inherit salvation?*

The question in v.13 is rhetorical. It demands a strong negative answer, so that a positive translation could read, *"But He (God) <u>never said to any angel at any time</u>, 'Sit on my right hand until I make your enemies your footstool': angels are merely ministering spirits, etc. ..."* The quotation is from Psalm 110:1 (a Psalm which is important to the Book of Hebrews since it deals with Christ's session and high priestly ministry in the order of Melchizedek).

   1.The place of Christ's Session: at God's right hand, v.13a

    "Sit at my right hand" involves the incarnate Christ in session, elevated far above all principalities and powers and every name that is named, Eph. 1:20-22. (A read-out on Christ's ministries in session is provided at the end of chapter one.)

    -**"sitting"** indicates that His earthly work is complete, His responsibilities in the work of redemption accomplished. The allusion is to once a job is done, one sits.

    - **"at my right hand"**, the place of dignity, exaltation, prestige, and power in the universe. The position has been won by virtue of His righteous essence and His work on the Cross: moreover, it assures the accomplishments of His future dealings, particularly the subjugation of His enemies.

   2. The duration of Christ's Session: until the Second Advent, v.13b

- ***"until I make your enemies your footstool"***: His enemies are all they who will not have Him to rule over them; included are fallen angels as well as humans. Operation Footstool will climax in the second advent vividly described in Rev. 19:11-20:6 (one should note the use of the word "angels" there). Hebrews 10:13 states that Christ waits *"expectantly,"* meaning, with eager anticipation for this momentous occasion in earth history.

3. The serving ministry of angels, v.14

- ***"angels are ministering spirits"***: while Christ sits in honor, angels serve.

- ***"sent forth unto ministry"***: the verb *"sent forth"* is present tense indicating continuous missions under the direction of God. *"Ministry"* is διακονια / *diakonia*, a term that covers various kinds of service or helps (same source for our word "deacon").

- ***"unto the heirs of salvation"***: elect angels serve believers! And they do so now, in this age! The specifics are not stated, but involved are helps, spiritual ministries, protection, watch-care. These unseen, but powerful beings, are God's emissaries for the good of Christ's brethren. *"Salvation"* is used here in the sense of our final, future deliverance from the sin nature, which will be accomplished when we receive our glorified bodies at the Rapture.

Conclusion to Chapter One: the transcendent majesty of the Son and God's message to mankind through Him demands earnest heed. Other messengers, prophets and angelic mediators, were preliminary: their message was important, but incomplete without Him. His message is final, absolute, and totally complete. Undue regard for angels on the part of the readers due to perverted Judaism and philosophic speculations is thus corrected: moreover, the reader is prepared for the focus of the Book: Christ.

The following summary is intended to illustrate the author's contrast between Christ and angels in Hebrews 1:6-14.

The Son as Messiah	Angels
-v.6 worshipped (by angels)	-v.6 worshippers of the Son
-addressed by God the Father as	
	-v.7 made ministering spirits by God
v.8 "God"	
v.8 a sovereign ruler	
v.8 a righteous ruler	
v.10 "Lord"	
v.10 Creator	
v.11 Immutable,	

This theme will continue in 2:5-18, but first the author exhorts the readers to pay special heed to the message of salvation in Christ in 2:1-4, the focus of our next section.

Parenthetical: Four Ministries of the Ascended Christ

Christ <u>seated</u> at the right hand of the Majesty on high focuses on His finished work at Calvary. That aspect of His ministry is finished, hence He is seated or at rest. But in this exalted position, He still "ministers" and functions in several capacities all of which relate to the Church and/or Believers of this age.

1. The ministry of HEADSHIP over the Church, Eph. 1:22,23; Col. 1:18; 2:19.

He is head of His Church which is His Body. This headship is both real and organic. As the head is the center and source of function for the physical body, so is Christ for His spiritual body, the Church.

2. The ministry of BESTOWER of spiritual gifts to the Body of Christ, Eph. 4:7-11; Rom. 12:3-8.

These gifts originate with the Head and are distributed to believers by the Holy Spirit so that the Body will function and grow in harmony with Christ. The entire doctrine of spiritual gifts is in view.

3. The ministry of INTERCESSOR, Heb. 7:25; Rom. 8:34.

In view is Christ's high priestly function in meeting the weaknesses and immature aspects of the Believer. He ever lives to make intercession for us who believe the Gospel, hence He is able to save us to the uttermost in time and degree.

4. The ministry of ADVOCATE, I John 2:1.

Again, the priestly representation of the Believer before God is in view: Christ is our advocate or lawyer, thus guaranteeing our absolute security before the Father.

HEBREWS 2:1-4

The infinite worthiness of Christ, the Messiah, the Son of God is a theme of Hebrews 1. In chapter 2, the major emphasis is on the necessity of His humanity (2:5-18), but first the author exhorts the readers to pay special attention to God's message in His Son (2:1-4). The emphases run something like this:

1:1-13	2:1-4	2:5-18
God's final message is His Son, the Messiah, who is Deity	Exhortation not to drift from God's message in His Son	The necessity for the humanity of the Son, the Messiah

There are at least five exhortation-warning sections interspersed throughout the Book (2:1-4; 3:7-4:16; 5:11-6:12, 10:19-39; 12:12-13:17). These must be interpreted in view of the fact that these Hebrew Christians were:

(1) desiring or in danger of desiring to escape hostility and persecutions heaped upon them by their families and fellow-nationals;

(2) under the influence of seducing propagandists of perverted Judaism <u>tempting them from Christ to religion</u>;

(3) being temped from the faith-way to the sight-way: i.e., to go back to the temple sacrificial system;

(4) secure in Christ since it is God that justifies (Rom. 8:33): i.e., they could not lose their salvation.

With these in mind, let us move on to the first exhortation-warning, 2:1-4: the danger of drifting from God's message in His Son.

I. Exhortation: heed the message in Messiah, the Son, v.1-3a

2:1 *Therefore we must give the more earnest heed to the things we have heard, lest we drift away.*

A. Basis for the exhortation, v.1a (<u>relates to Divine Provision</u>)

"Therefore" translates *dia touto* (διὰ τουτο), more literally "because of this": i.e., because of the declared glories of the Son in chapter 1, *"we must give the more earnest heed..."*

B. The exhortation, v.1b (<u>relates to Human Responsibility</u>)

1. *"PAY ATTENTION"*

"...we must give the more earnest heed": the verb *must give* and the infinitive *heed* are both in the present tense, signifying durative action, that is "on and on" attention to the message. Our occupation with Christ and

God's message in Him is vital. It is worthy of our attention and necessary to our mental attitudes at all times. Note that the author includes himself in the exhortation ("__we__ ought to give the more earnest heed").

2. *"to the things which we heard"*

This relates to the message of salvation through the Son.

3. *"lest we drift away"* (KJV, "lest we should let them slip")

The verb is (aorist t., active v., subjunctive m.*) from *pararreo* (παραρρεω), "to flow by", "to glide aside", or "to drift away": the idea is that of being swept past a sure anchorage that is within reach. By application: these Jewish believers are in danger of drifting by the great truths of salvation in Christ or attempting to live life without paying attention to the significance of salvation. In verse 3, this is spoken of as *"neglecting salvation"*, that is, being careless in regards to the doctrines of salvation and their personal application. The mechanics are not discussed, but neglect of Bible study, quenching the Holy Spirit, lack of faith-rest techniques, etc., certainly apply. Note again that the author includes himself in the admonition ("lest __we__ should drift away").

The tendency of modern day Christianity is to ignore doctrine and focus on human experience as though experience were the criterion of truth. In the early church, believers were taught doctrine and were encouraged to interpret experience in the light of doctrine. <u>The warning here relates to the danger of drifting by the doctrine!</u>

C. Stimulus to obey the exhortation: the firmness of the Old Covenant, v. 2

   2:2 *For if the word spoken through angels proved steadfast, and every transgression and disobedience received a just reward,...*

A very literal reading: *"for if* (1st class condition) *the through- angels-having-been-spoken-word was steadfast or inviolable and every transgression and disobedience received just recompense..."*

<u>Two key ideas are in view:</u>

1. The Old Covenant mediated partially through angels was fixed or unalterable.

   "Steadfast" (βεβαιος / *bebaios*) means "firm", or "fixed" in the sense of being unalterable. Now if that mediated through angels was firm or unchangeable, what of that mediated through God's very own Son! Angelic mediation is spoken of in Acts 7:53 and Gal. 3:19. Judaism of New Testament times made far more of angelic mediation than God intended.

2. The Old Covenant carried with it a fixed retribution.

- ***"transgression"*** (παραβασις / *parabasis*) is disobedience due to obstinence: the   word means "a stepping by the side"; it describes a very willful, overt act of direct disobedience.

- ***"disobedience"*** (παρακοη / *parakoē*) is dereliction due to slothfulness or neglect to hear what God is saying. Negligence is the source of this type of disobedience.

- ***"just recompense"*** means that the punishment suited the transgression, not the transgressor. The system was objective, therefore just.

D. Stimulus to obey the exhortation (cont'd.): the Great Salvation, v. 3a

2:3 *how shall we escape if we neglect so great a salvation...*

1. The <u>So Great Salvation</u>

"Salvation" is the liberating message in Christ: that of deliverance from sin for believing sinners. The entire salvation package is in view: Phase 1, Justification (permanent deliverance from the penalty of sin), Phase 2 Sanctification (deliverance from the power of sin in the present), and Phase 3, Glorification (deliverance from the presence of sin in the future). (See Illustration #2, page 23).

The salvation is "so great" because of:

- the greatness of its source: God, who planned salvation

- the greatness of its sacrifice: the Son, the Christ, who executed the plan

- the greatness of its effect: absolute and total forgiveness for the believing sinner.

These aspects of salvation are persistent themes of Hebrews.

2. The Danger of Neglecting the So Great Salvation

<u>A clarifying translation</u>: *"How shall <u>we ourselves</u> escape if being careless of so great salvation?"*

The subject (we) is emphatic: once again the author includes himself. To neglect the saving message is to be careless or negligent regarding it: the participle is aorist tense* of *ameleo* (αμελεω) used in a conditional sense, hence *"if being careless..."* There are some things in life about which one can be careless or negligent without disastrous consequences, but to so respond to God's salvation in Christ leads to serious consequences that cannot be escaped.

Believers can never be condemned (John 5:24; I Cor. 11:32), but they certainly can expect discipline for carelessness or neglect of God's grace. His discipline is the subject of 12:3-15 where these very Hebrew Christians are encouraged to **"look diligently lest any come short of the grace of God"**; this *"grace"* is

directly related to child training and in no way applicable to an unbeliever. Believers are not to stiff-arm the grace of God!

Unbelievers stand condemned (John 3:18). Both the context and the author's inclusion of himself in this warning indicate that it is addressed to believers.

II. Fact: communication and confirmation of the Great Salvation, v.3b-4

A. The original pronouncement: spoken by the Lord Jesus, v.3b

2:3b ***which at the first began to be spoken by the Lord, and was confirmed to us by those who heard Him,***

Christ persistently taught the need of every man to believe on Him for personal salvation. The message of forgiveness in the Old Testament is largely in types, foreshadows, and sacrifices. But when Messiah came on the scene, the gospel focused entirely on Him and His cross work, the reality to which the Old Testament types and shadows pointed. His is the body that cast the Old Testament shadows.

B. The convincing confirmation, v.3c

"Confirmed" translates *bebaioo* (βεβαιοω) (in the aorist, passive, indicative*), which means "to make firm" or "steadfast" (noun form in v.2). God bore witness by means of supernatural proofs that accompanied the disciples' verbal pronouncements. This witness made the message firm, secure, solid. In other words, God's purpose in the miracles that accompanied the Apostolic Age was to substantiate the verbal message so that listeners, particularly Jewish listeners, would take notice that the message indeed was His.

Note that the writer includes himself with those who received the gospel from others secondhand. This is one of the strongest arguments <u>against Pauline authorship</u>. Paul insisted that he got the gospel directly from Jesus Christ (Gal. 1:11-18) and not through anyone else.

C. The Divine means of confirmation: miracle-type gifts, v.4

2:4 ***God also bearing witness both with signs and wonders, with various miracles, and gifts of the Holy Spirit, according to His own will?***

The construction is genitive absolute of <u>means</u>, hence translated "confirmed unto us by them that heard **by means of God bearing witness** with them by signs and wonders, etc."

1. signs (σημειον / *semeion*): miracles that call attention to the essence of something (when used with Christ, the miracle calls attention to His Deity; see John 2:11, 4:54, 6:14).

2. wonders (τερας / *teras*): miracles with attention on the effect they have on those who observe them or hear of them.

3. powers (δυναμις / *dunamis*): miracles or displays that highlight God's unique and inherent power.

4. gifts of the Holy Spirit (μερισμος / *merismos*): unique impartations or distributions by the Holy Spirit in accord with His sovereign will.

All these witness to the Great Salvation: they are testimonies to the Divine nature, mission, and sacrifice of Christ. They substantiate that the Great Salvation is from God! <u>The primary purpose of miracles in the first century was not to alleviate suffering</u>, rather to substantiate the verbal presentation of the Gospel.

<u>Conclusion</u>: in view of the greatness of salvation, these Hebrew Christians are encouraged to heed all aspects of its message. God Himself confirmed its veracity by the miraculous gifts of the Holy Spirit that accompanied the Apostolic Age (the first century).

Figure #2: The "So Great Salvation" In Three Tenses or Stages

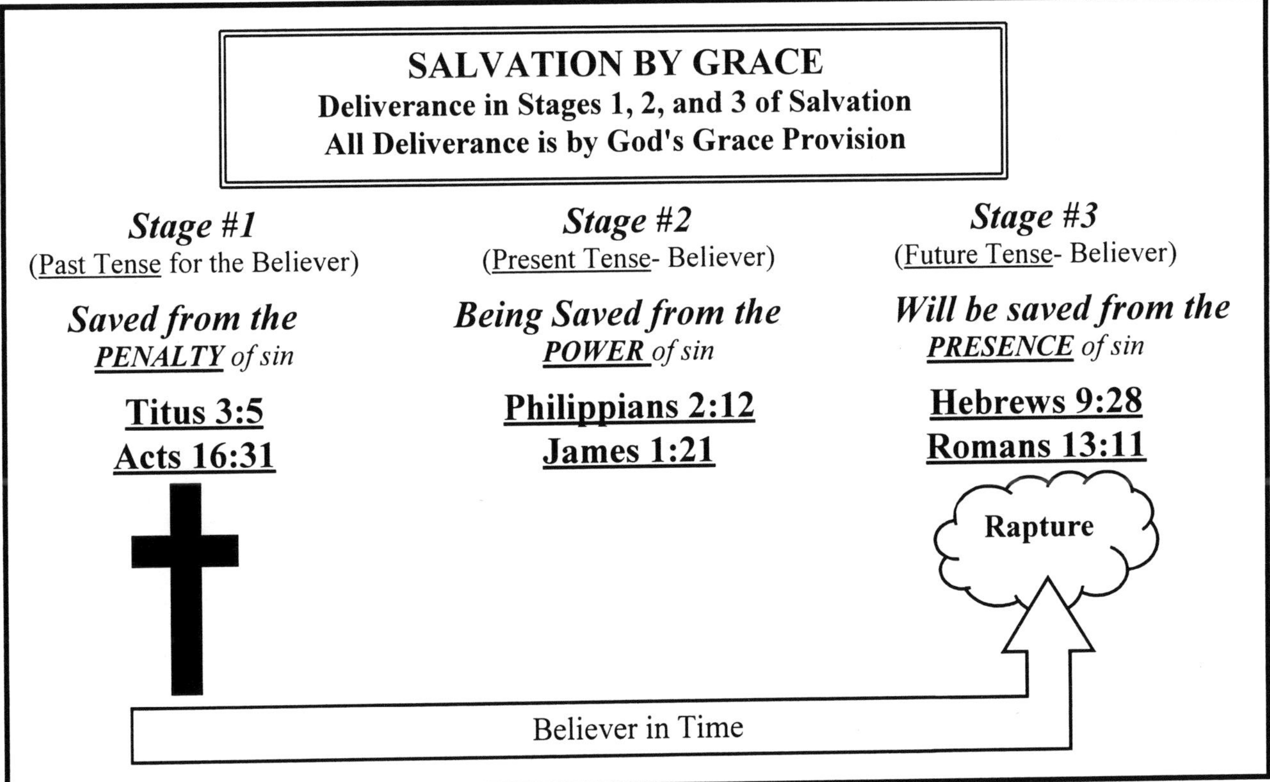

EXPLANATION: SALVATION, THE DELIVERANCE FROM SIN AND ITS EFFECTS, IS A GIFT. IT IS A PACKAGE DEAL. IT IS TOTALLY BY GRACE (EPH.2: 8-9). GRACE MEANS THAT GOD PROVIDES WHAT IS NECESSARY FOR EVERY PHASE OR STAGE OF SALVATION. MAN APPROPRIATES WHAT GOD PROVIDES BY FAITH; THAT IS, MAN PUTS HIS FAITH OR TRUST TOTALLY IN WHAT GOD PROVIDES FOR EACH TENSE OF SALVATION. THIS IS WHAT PAUL MEANS IN EPH. 2:8-9: "FOR BY GRACE YOU HAVE BEEN SAVED

THROUGH FAITH… IT IS THE GIFT OF GOD, NOT OF WORKS LEST ANY MAN SHOULD BOAST."

HEBREWS 2:5-18

In this portion, the author is led by the Holy Spirit to give five reasons for the Son taking humanity to Himself:

I.   That He should taste death for every man and thus bring many into glory, v.5-13;

II.   That He might destroy Satan, the one who had the power over death, v.14;

III.   That He might free men from the fear of death, v.15;

IV.   That He might become a merciful and faithful high priest, v.17; and

V.   That He might make propitiation for the sins of the people (a subsidiary purpose of His priesthood), v.17.

I. Reason #1: <u>Christ became man</u> to win back for man dominion over the inhabited earth: this required His substitutionary death for every man, v. 5-13.

The following points seek to highlight the author's logic or thought structure in this extended paragraph.

A. Authority (dominion) over the future world: not to angels but to Christ, v.5.

> **2:5 *For He has not put the world to come, of which we speak, in subjection to angels.***

<u>A literal translation</u>: *"For not to angels did He subject the inhabited earth which is to come, about which we are speaking."*

The inhabited earth (οικουμενη / *oikoumenē*) to come refers to the Millennial Kingdom: <u>it will not be under</u> the subjection of angels. Though angels exercise great influence presently, and though they are now more powerful creatures than men, they will not control the earth to come. No doubt the Millennial Kingdom on earth is in view: the Second Coming to establish this was referred to in 1:6. Angels will not administrate; Christ will.

In verse 5, the author is simply preparing us for what is to follow, all of which is intended to help us appreciate the prolific effects and values of the cross of Christ. The logic runs as follows:

- Authority over the inhabited earth to come is not committed to angels, v.5;

- Authority over the original earth was committed to man, v.6-8a;

- Authority was lost, since it is obvious that all things are not now under man, v.8b;

- Authority is regained in Christ, who died, but is now alive and above all, v.9;

- Christ shares this glory with those who are His, v.10-13.

- <u>Summary</u>: authority over the inhabited earth to come will be in the hands of Jesus, the Christ, and those that are His.

The word "for" in v.5 ties the verse to the previous context: God bore witness to the Gospel with miraculous signs and wonders because these powers are exemplary of the power of the One who will rule the inhabited earth to come, the Lord Jesus Christ. What a marvelous substantiation 2:5 and 1:6 are to the fact of the coming, literal reign of Christ over planet earth! The authority of Christ in the world of the future is a pre-determined fact in the mind of God.

2:1-4 states that the great deliverance (salvation) has begun. We are not to ignore it, for the same Christ that brought salvation in His First Advent will return again to rule the world to come! Οικουμενη / *oikoumenē*(v. 5) views the world as man's habitation (a civilization) in distrinction to αεον / *aeon* which sees it from the standpoint of time (an age) and κοσμος / *kosmos* which sees it from its inner coherence (a system, an organized mentality, an outlook).

"Subject" or "put in subjection" (aorist t., active v., indicative m.*) is from υποτασσω / *hupotasso*, a military term for the dominion, authority, and order involved in the military chain of command. It is repeated in v.8.

> B. Authority (dominion) over the present world: originally given to man (Adam), v.6-8a
>
> > **2:6-8a *But one testified in a certain place, saying: "What is man that You are mindful of him, Or the son of man that You take care of him? 7 You have made him a little lower than the angels; You have crowned him with glory and honor, And set him over the works of Your hands. a You have put all things in subjection under his feet."***
>
> > <u>A literal translation</u>: *"But one has testified somewhere saying, 'What is man that You remember him? Or the son of man that You closely observe him? You made him less for a little than the angels. You have crowned him with glory and honor. You appointed him over the works of Your hands. You have put all things in subjection under his feet.'"*
>
> > At least <u>5 facts of man's authority</u> in the Divine design are in view in this passage (a quote of Psalm 8:4-6 from the LXX):
>
> > 1. God is mindful of and intensely interested in man (v.6)
> >
> > > The Psalmist is astonished by the dignity afforded man from Divine viewpoint: he is aware that all are sinners and rebels against God, yet God remains concerned for man's welfare. *"Closely observe"* (KJV, "visitest") translates επισκεπτομαι / *episkeptomai*, "to carefully observe, to inspect with great care": involved is the idea of great interest and desire to aid.
>
> > 2. God made man, for a little while, lower than angels (v.6a)
> >
> > > *"for a little"* (βραχυ/ *brachu*) anticipates man's exaltation in Christ above the angelic sphere. <u>He is lower than angels only for a little time</u>. In Christ, he is presently seated in the heavenlies far above the angelic sphere, Eph. 1:20; 2:6.
>
> > 3. God crowned man (Adam) with glory and honor (v.7b)

The Psalmist is amazed by the honor and estimate of man's station in the Divine scheme of things.

4. God set or placed man (Adam) over the lesser creation, (v.7c)

In view is God's stated goal for man in the original creative acts, Gen. 1:28: "*and God said unto them, 'Be fruitful and multiply and replenish the earth and subdue it: and <u>have</u> <u>dominion</u> (* רָדָה */ radah) over the fish of the sea and over the fowl of the air, and over every living thing that moveth upon the earth.'*" Psalm 8:6 supports this: "*You <u>made</u> him <u>to</u> <u>have dominion</u>* (hiphil stem of מָשַׁל / *mashal*: i.,e., causative action) *over the* works of Thy hands."

5. God put all things earth-wise in subjection to man (v.8a).

This is a summary statement of man's (Adam's) original position in the Divine order: though lower than angels, he was intended to rule over planet earth and the lesser creation. <u>To this point, man is portrayed as dominant, in charge of things</u>. The last clause in v.8, however, indicates that something happened to thwart the purposes of God, for "<u>*now*</u> *we do not yet see all things under him.*"

C. Authority (dominion) by man not realized (8c).

2:8b,c *You have put all things in subjection under his feet." For in that He put all in subjection under him, He left nothing that is not put under him. But now we do not yet see all things put under him.*

<u>Translation emphasis</u>: "*But <u>now</u>, we see not <u>yet</u> all things subjected to him.*"

Instead of man being over, he is normally under! In his efforts to rule in planet earth, he faces one crises after another – human relations crises, economic crises, environmental crises, energy crises, moral crises! Why: Because man's position in the Divine design was/is marred by sin. Adam belied God's trust and lost his dominion over creation. Sin and death entered and man became more dominated than dominant. However, this did not mean the frustration of God's purposes: the forfeited dominion would be regained by the Son taking humanity to Himself, paying the redemptive price of death for mankind, and defeating Satan in his own territory of death (v. 9-15).

D. Authority (dominion) regained by Christ, v.9

2:9 *But we see Jesus, who was made a little lower than the angels, for the suffering of death crowned with glory and honor, that He, by the grace of God, might taste death for everyone.*

A literal translation: "*But we see Jesus, the One having been made for a little while lower than angels that by the grace of God He might taste death for every man, having been crowned with glory and honor.*"

1. <u>the Incarnation fact</u>: "Jesus, the One made for a little while lower than angels."

Note the use of Christ's human name, *Jesus.* In view is the eternal Son who took to Himself humanity by being born of the Virgin Mary: He who created the angels and ruled over them took our frame and thus became lower than angels in His humanity, but only for a brief time.

2.   <u>the Incarnation purpose</u>:   *"that by the grace of God He might taste death for* (ὑπερ / *huper, in the interest of, in the stead of*) *every man."*

Christ not only took to Himself our frame, He also took what was due us, death, and by this redeemed us from death's curse. Note:

- the ultimate source of salvation = the Grace of God

- the procuring cause of salvation = the death of Christ

- the Divine direction of salvation = for every man

Passages that teach that Christ's death was substitutionary, that is, that He took to Himself the death that every sinner deserved, are Isa. 53:6, 11,12; Gal. 3:13; 1Cor. 15:3; 2Cor. 5:21: 1Pet. 2:24, 3:18; Titus 2:14; Heb. 2:9, etc. (There are many more, of course).

Passages that teach that the substitutionary death of Christ was for <u>all men</u> are: I John 2:2; I Tim. 2:6; Heb. 2:9, 10:12; 2Pet. 3:18; 2Cor. 5:14,19; Rom. 5:18.

3.   <u>the exaltation of the Incarnate Christ</u>: *"because of the suffering of the death having been crowned with glory and honor."*

The suffering of death is the ground for the Lord's exaltation in His humanity. The participle *"crowned"* (εστεφανωμενον / *estephanōmenon*) is perfect tense, passive voice*, calling attention to the abiding results of God's action in glorifying Jesus. Jesus now sits in the position of honor and glory at God's right hand (1:3). There He is positioned for ruler-ship over the universe; all authority is His (Mt. 28:18). He is awaiting the inevitable demise of all of His enemies (1:13) at which time the cosmos will experience His absolute authority (Rev. 19:11ff.). At the right hand of God is the man Christ Jesus, far above the angelic sphere, far superior to angels. And, glorious truth, saved humanity shares with Him this exalted position and status (Eph. 1:21; 2:6)!

The author is underscoring the fact that the unique suffering and death of Messiah was part of the Divine design in winning back the glory and honor that Adam lost. Moreover, <u>Adam at his best was lower than angels</u>: whereas, <u>in Christ, humanity that was lost is raised to a far superior position than angels</u>. How gloriously does God bring to naught the designs of our arch-foe, Satan!

V.9 marks a turning point in the argument the author is presenting: now in v. 10-13, he supports the concept that Messiah had to suffer to accomplish God's plan for mankind.

    E. Final authority for all of this, v.10

2:10 *For it was fitting for Him, for whom are all things and by whom are all things, in bringing many sons to glory, to make the captain of their salvation perfect through sufferings.*

<u>A literal translation</u>: *"for it was fitting for Him, because of whom (are) all things and through whom are all things, in leading many sons into glory, to perfect the author of their salvation through sufferings."*

That Christ would be perfected by sufferings was fitting or commensurate with God, who is both Lord and Creator of all things: it is compatible with His essence and character, and it was necessary in bringing sons into glory.

1. **God's plan in view**: "because of whom…and through whom are all things…

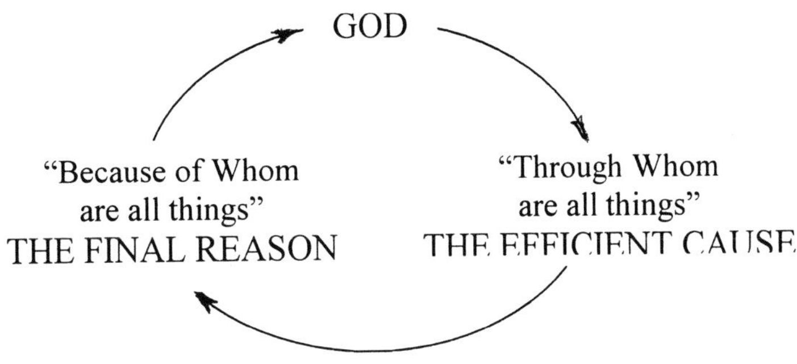

God is seen both as the source and the final end of all.

Col. 1:16 states the same idea about Christ: *"…all things were created through Him and for Him"*! Christ is seen as both the source and end of all!

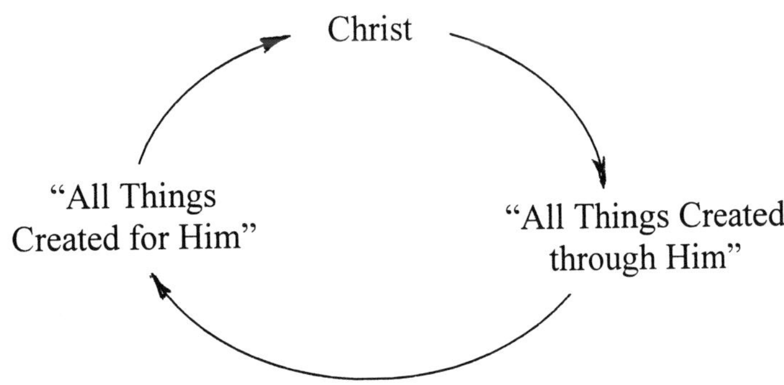

2. **God's work in view**: *"in leading many sons into glory"*

"Sons" are Believers, of course: they are in relationship with God by grace as is a son to a father. These sons share the "glory" attached to the Son, the Lord Jesus Christ.

3. **Christ's work in view:** *"to make the author of their salvation perfect through sufferings."*

"Author", αρχηγος / *archēgos*, means the originator, the leader, the trailblazer: it is used again in 12:2 where He is called *"the author (archēgos) and finisher of our faith."* Christ is the One who leads or goes before in the matter of our salvation. He was first to go through death and the first to be glorified. As such, He is the originator and trailblazer of our salvation.

For Christ to be functionally perfect in this role as well as that of our glorified High Priest, it was necessary that He experience suffering as a man (2:17,18; 5:7-9).
Christ's sufferings reached their consummation in the cross where, under Divine judgment, He volitionally became the expiatory sacrifice for the sins of mankind.

4. **Man's benefit in view:** *"...He is not ashamed to call them 'Brethren'"*

2:11 *For both He who sanctifies and those who are being sanctified are all of one, for which reason He is not ashamed to call them brethren,*

Verse 11 gives added support for the "fitness" of the Divine design of Christ's sufferings. Both Christ, the Sanctifier, and Believers, the sanctified or set-apart ones, have one common source: God the Father. Thus, our Lord has no reservation in calling us His brothers. The effectiveness of our being set-apart or sanctified in Christ is dramatically expressed in Hebrews 10:10; **"By the which will (God's will), we are having been sanctified <u>once for all</u> through the offering of the body of Jesus Christ"** (the verb "having been sanctified" is a perfect periphrastic*: the author could not have used stronger language!).

Verses 12 and 13 are three quotations from the Old Testament (Psalm 22:22; Isa. 8:17,18 from LXX) that confirm the statement of v.11.

2:12-13 *saying: "I will declare Your name to My brethren; In the midst of the assembly I will sing praise to You." 13 And again: "I will put My trust in Him." And again: "Here am I and the children whom God has given Me."*

<u>Conclusion</u>: verses 5-13 state that the Son became man to win back for man dominion over the inhabited earth. This required His substitutionary death. Moreover, He became perfect or complete for His role as the file leader of salvation and as an empathetic High Priest by the things He suffered. He did not die as a martyr: the suffering of His cross was part of the Divine design and totally necessary for the bringing of many sons into glory. This glory will be manifested when He returns to rule the inhabited earth (1:6; 2:5).

Having explained reason #1 for the Son becoming human or taking to Himself humanity, the author now states in rapid-fire four more reasons.

II. Reason #2: Christ became man that He might render powerless the one having the power of death, the Devil, v.14. This required His own death.

2:14 *Inasmuch then as the children have partaken of flesh and blood, He Himself likewise shared in the same, that through death He might destroy him who had the power of death, that is, the devil,*

A literal translation: *"Since then the children have in common flesh and blood, He Himself also took part with the same in a similar manner, in order that through the death He might make ineffective the one having the power of death, that is the Devil."*

The logic runs as follows:

A. **The human problem or condition:** *"... the children have in common a flesh and blood nature."*

Flesh and blood is a Hebrew idiom for the nature of man. The verb "have in common" (perfect t., active v., indicative m.*) from κοινωνεω / koioneo, meaning, men's flesh- blood nature was permanent and could not be shaken. Their flesh- blood nature into which they were locked necessitated His.

B. **The Incarnation:** *"therefore Christ Himself* (very emphatic) *took part with the same in a similar manner."*

Interestingly, the author now changes verbs: "took part" translates μετεσχεν/ meteschen, "to hold with," "to have with," "to take part with." The idea is that Christ voluntarily took to Himself a human frame, a human essence, in conjunction with His Deity. The hypostatic union is in view: undiminished Deity and perfect humanity in the person of Messiah (Philippians 2:5-9 explains the process). The overriding purpose of the Incarnation was to make possible His substitutionary death for mankind.

"In similar manner" means that Christ came into the human race similarly as others: He was born as a baby (though uniquely through the virgin birth).

C. **The solution to humanity's dilemma:** *"that through the death, He might render powerless the one having the power of the death, the Devil."*

His taking a human body could not accomplish redemption: only the giving up of His life in death could.

"That He might render inoperative" translates καταργεω/ *katargeō*, "to make ineffective," "to make idle," "to put out of business." Christ died to put the Devil out of business, to render him powerless!

Note that Satan has (present participle) the power or dominion (κρατος / *kratos*) of death, not power over death. He rules in the death realm as illustrated below.

Figure #3 The Devil's Current Dominion

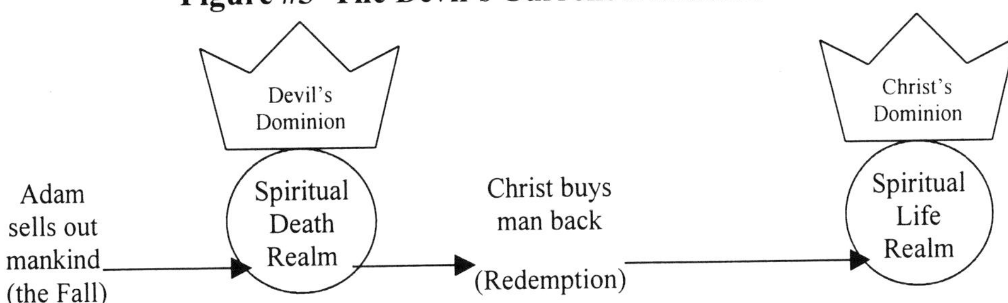

The teaching is this:

- Satan was not annihilated at the cross.

- Satan's power was broken in the Spiritual death realm at the cross.

- Spiritual death cannot hold the person who puts his faith in the Savior.

- Physical death cannot keep the body in the grave.

- In conquering death, Jesus brought to naught the Devil.

III. Reason #3: Christ became man to free men from the fear of death, v.15,16.

A. Purpose stated, v.15

2:15 *and release those who through fear of death were all their lifetime subject to bondage.*

The fear of death is the effect of sin. Death is a concept that confuses and overwhelms the mind of the unsaved. The terrors involved in death lead to bondage, but Christ has removed the terror of death for the Believer (1Cor. 15:55-58; Rom. 8:15,21).

B. Purpose to help mankind reaffirmed, v.16

2:16 *For indeed He does not give aid to angels, but He does give aid to the seed of Abraham.*

<u>A literal translation</u>: *"for without doubt, he is not laying hold of angels* (to help them), *but of the seed of Abraham he is laying hold* (to help)."

1. Both verbs are present t., middle v., indicative m.*: the help goes on and on (present t.) and He is intensely interested in the results (middle voice).

2. Angels are by-passed: they are locked into their negative volition. Those angels who fell, fell irretrievably.

3. It is the spiritual seed of Abraham (those who believe on Him) that He secures and helps. The entire family of faith is in view as per Gal. 3:7, "they that are of faith, the same are the Sons of Abraham." His death frees them from the

power of death and His resurrection life assures them of the faithful, durative discharge of His High Priestly ministries.

IV. Reason #4: Christ became man in order to serve Believers as a merciful and faithful High Priest, v.17a.

2:17 *Therefore, in all things He had to be made like His brethren, that He might be a merciful and faithful High Priest in things pertaining to God,*

<u>A literal translation</u>: *"Therefore, He was bound* (obliged) *to be made like His brethren in all things in order that He might become a merciful and faithful High Priest in the things pertaining to God."*

Two major functions of the High Priest are in view: (1) intercession or representing man to God and (2) communication or representing God to man. Jesus Christ as the God-man is perfectly suited for both responsibilities: He perfectly mediates between man and God. V. 17 refers to His God-ward responsibilities: v.18, His man-ward. See Figure #4.

Figure #4 Christ as the Perfect High Priest Mediator

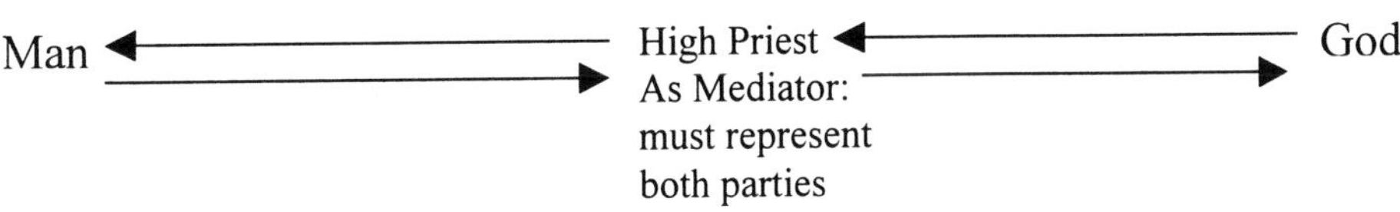

The High Priestly ministries of Christ are a vital subject of this letter (2:17,18; 3:1,2; 4:14-16; 5:1-10; 7:1-9:24).

V. Reason #5: Christ became man in order to make propitiation for sins, v.17b-18

2:17b,18 *to make propitiation for the sins of the people. 18 For in that He Himself has suffered, being tempted, He is able to aid those who are tempted.*

The KJV and the NIV *incorrectly* translate ιλασκεσθαι (*hilaskesthai*) "reconciliation". This verb and all its cognates always relate to propitiation, not reconciliation.

Propitiation means to atone for or to make expiatory satisfaction for sins: the key idea is the removal of guilt by a satisfactory offering. The Son took to Himself humanity so as to satisfy God's righteous demands by offering Himself as a propitiatory or expiatory sacrifice for sins. Propitiation is always God-ward. Reconciliation is always man-ward.

A. Christ's High Priestly work in relation to God, **PROPITIATION**, v.17b.

Key thoughts on <u>propitiation</u>:

1. God stipulates that which propitiates both in the Old Testament and in the New Testament: the initiative in this matter is always ascribed to His grace, Lev. 17:11; Rom. 3:25.

2. "Hilasterion", "the place of propitiation," was the mercy seat, the covering of the Ark of the Covenant, in Old Testament times (hilasterion is actually translated "mercy seat" in Heb. 9:5). The ritual surrounding the mercy seat symbolically represented how God dealt with His people's sin then, Lev. 17.

3. But the death of Christ is how God <u>really</u> deals with sin (no symbolism, here), Rom. 3:25. "Propitiation" is "set forth", "proposed publicly" as opposed to the hidden, symbolical aspects of Old Testament atonement at the mercy seat.

4. The propitiatory death of Christ is at once the vindication of God's righteousness and justice and the salvation of the believing sinner. Propitiation means God is satisfied. His holiness, righteousness and justice are in no way threatened when He forgives sin on the basis of Christ's death. In propitiation, God is not saying to the sinner, "I am satisfied with you;" rather, "I am forever satisfied with my Son who met my demands upon sin in His cross." *Propitiation* means God is satisfied. Human beings express their satisfaction by personal faith in the work of Christ for them in His Cross.

5. The universality of Christ's propitiation is expressed in I John 2:2, *"He is the propitiation for our sins and not for ours only, but also for the sins of the whole world."* The key issue that men must face is believing that God really did make propitiation in the death of His Son: unbelief here is the one sin that condemns (John 16:8,11).

B. Christ's High Priestly ministry in relation to man: **HELP**, v.18

The thought movement of v.18 is as follows:

1. He Himself suffered via testings under the same conditions of humanity. He was born, He grew up, He matured, He worked, slept, thirsted, hungered, He died. He went through the entire gamut of human experience and testing.

2. He was without sin in all of this, 4:15

3. He was made perfect or complete for His role as a merciful and faithful High Priest through suffering, 2:10; 5:8,9

4. He is now serving as High Priest, 7:23-28

5. Therefore, He is able to help us, 2:18. The word <u>help</u> (βοεθησαι / *boethēesai*) means "to run to the aid of one in distress." The idea is that He can perform in His High Priestly glory and power all that is necessary to aid, keep, and preserve the sons of God: He can save them to the uttermost (7:25).

Conclusion and summary of 2:5-18

The persistent theme that runs through this paragraph is the necessity for the humanity of God's Son.

- By that means He would suffer an expiatory death for men (v.9) and thus be crowned with glory and honor by God, v. 9.

- By that means He would be the author of salvation and bring many sons to glory, v.10.

- By that means He would be subjected to human sufferings and thus be perfected for His various and necessary ministries to His Brethren, v.10, 18.

- By that means He would bring Satan to naught and put him out of business, v.14.

- By that means He would deliver God's children from death to freedom and become their merciful and faithful High Priest, v.15-18.

Such a One deserves due consideration and careful thought! Chapter 3 will begin with an exhortation to so consider Him.

Hebrews 3:1-6

Having mentioned Christ as our merciful High Priest (2:17,18), the writer now requests a serous consideration of His faithfulness over God's house. Christ not only built God's house (in which Moses served), He also rules over it. He can be depended upon. His High Priestly ministries of mediation, intercession, and help for Believers are in view.

The key emphases to this point are:

- Chapter 1 describes God's Son who took humanity to Himself, purged our sins, and sits at God's right hand waiting to rule the world: EMPHASIS – DEITY.

- Chapter 2 tells why God's Son became human: to pay the death penalty for sin for every man, to conquer death through His death, to put Satan out of business, and to serve believers faithfully in this age as High Priest: EMPHASIS – HUMANITY.

- Chapter 3a is an appeal to consider Christ as the faithful High Priest over God's house: EMPHASIS – HELP FOR BELIEVERS.

Hebrews 3:1-6, A Command to Consider Our High Priest

The introductory *"therefore"* reaches back into chapter 2: that is, because Christ has taken to Himself our frame and because He is now faithfully serving as our High Priest before God, we should <u>therefore</u> give intensive consideration of Him in that role.

I. Those called to (to consider Him), v.1a.

3:1a *Therefore, holy brethren, partakers of the heavenly calling,*

A. **"holy brethren"**

- **"holy"** translates ἅγιος / *hagios*, which means "set apart" ones; that is set apart to God. Divine identity is in view.

God sees every Believer as "set apart" uniquely for Himself in Christ. Hebrews 10:10 emphatically states this as a final, once for all fact; *By that will* (God's will) *we have been sanctified through the offering of the body of Jesus Christ **once for all**.*

One does not become "holy" by human effort, rather by identity with Christ via faith.

- **"brethren"** emphasizes human identity: the term speaks of endearment, fellowship, and common bonds in Christ.

B. **"partakers of a heavenly calling"**

- **"partakers"** is μεταχοι / *metochoi*, "ones who hold something in common," "those who are partakers": the emphasis is on what is held, the thing held, rather than the sharing itself. It is used as follows in this Book:

1:9   Christ partook of the oil of gladness above all <u>others</u> (metochoi ones: above all who shared it)

3:1   Believers partake of the heavenly calling (as opposed to Israel's earthly calling).

3:14   Believers have become <u>partakers</u> of Christ: the verb "have become" is γινομαι/ *ginomai* in the perfect tense*, meaning they <u>permanently</u> partake of Christ. The emphasis is on the abiding results of the action.

6:4   Believers partake of the Holy Spirit

12:10 Believers partake of God's holiness.

It is obvious that those called to "consider" Jesus are believers. The command, then, is very applicable to all of us, even though the primary recipients of this letter were Jewish believers going through unique trials.

II. The Commandment, v.1b

3:1b *consider the Apostle and High Priest of our confession, Christ Jesus,*

A. Imperative: "consider" Jesus

This verb is the aorist active imperative* of κατανοεω / *katanoeō*, "to discern," "to perceive."   The prefixed preposition (kata) intensifies the action of the verb: "think seriously," "take thoroughly into account," "give intensive consideration" is the idea.

In planning a dinner for the President of the United States, one would *katanoeō*: he would carefully think through (like thinking through a wedding, or an addition to one's home). "Consider" Jesus: "think through His roles as Apostle and High Priest of what we believe," "consider the significance of all that He has been and currently is to the Father on our behalf."

B. Object of consideration: Jesus as:

1. "<u>The</u> Apostle of our confession" (earthly mission in view)

"Apostle" means "a sent one with a mission." It is articular, meaning, Jesus is <u>the</u> sent one: He is unique in His message and authority. Christ persistently taught that His words and His works were those of the Father from whom He was sent (John 3:31-35, words of John the Baptist: John 5:19,20, 36-38; 6:29; 7:28,29, words of Jesus).

"Of our confession" (ὁμολογια / *homologia*) means He is the one we confess or give verbal assent to. To confess means to "agree with" or "to say the same thing about." When we "confess Christ," we in essence are saying the same thing about Him that God does; we are agreeing with God about His Son.

2. "The High Priest of our confession" (heavenly mission in view).

As an apostle, He was sent forth to planet earth and having completed the Father's mission, He has gone back to heaven now to serve as High Priest ministering the will of the Father to Believers and representing them before the Father.

By application to the Hebrew-Christians: since Christ is now the Christian's High Priest and as such a fulfillment of the Old Testament types, do not be tempted to return to Judaism's High Priest. Give Christ due consideration in this regard, after all, it is part and parcel of what we confess or believe.

III. Support-stimuli for the command (the virtues of Christ), v.2-6

    A. Christ, faithful to God (like Moses), v.2

        3:2 *who was faithful to Him who appointed Him, as Moses also was faithful in all His house.*

The translation would best read, *"as being faithful to the One who appointed him as also Moses (was faithful) in all His house."* Christ <u>keeps on being faithful</u> (the participle [present tense]* is ωντα / *ōnta*): He keeps on serving. Christ's ministry is continual: Moses' was temporary. Moses' ministry was limited to the nation of Israel; Christ's, of course, is much broader and all encompassing as the next three verses attest.

    B. Christ, Superior to Moses, v.3-6a

        3:3-6a *For this One has been counted worthy of more glory than Moses, inasmuch as He who built the house has more honor than the house. 4 For every house is built by someone, but He who built all things is God. 5 And Moses indeed was faithful in all His house as a servant, for a testimony of those things which would be spoken afterward, 6 but Christ as a Son over His own house,*

Christ is compared to Moses in v.2. Now He is contrasted in an effort to show His intrinsic greatness.

	Christ	Moses
v.3	- Builder of God's house: the verb κατασκευαζω / *kataskeuazō* combines the ideas of founding, building and establishing. Christ is the author, the establisher of that which Moses was only a part of.	- simply a part of God's spiritual house
v.4	- Christ, as the One to whom all things owe their origin, is Deity (as per 1:3,10).	
v.5,6	- (a μεν /δε construction*)	- faithful as a servant <u>IN</u> Gods' house

<table>
<tr><td>

- While Moses was faithful <u>in</u> God's house as a servant, Christ as a Son is <u>OVER</u> or <u>RULES OVER</u> God's spiritual house. That a "greater than Moses" is here is left without doubt. Rather than disparage Moses, the author merely places him in proper relationship to Christ - thus directing veneration to the proper object.

</td><td>

Moses was merely a servant, one with high responsibilities: this is said to be "for or toward (εἰς) a testimony of the things spoken later" meaning: Moses merely witnessed in God's spiritual house in types and foreshadows that were later clarified in and by the person of Christ. Moses' ministry was preparatory: Christ's was final and absolute.

</td></tr>
</table>

IV. Qualification, v.6b

3:6b *whose house we are if* (3rd Class Condition*) *we hold fast the confidence and the rejoicing of the hope firm to the end.*

Clarification:

1. This verse does not teach that salvation or union with Christ depends upon maintaining confidence to the end. Anyone, who believes in Christ, Jew or Gentile, has everlasting life and shall never perish (John 10:28). The scriptures clearly teach that a believer can never be condemned by God (John 5:24; 1Cor. 11:32).

2. *"If we hold fast the confidence…"* is a 3rd Class Condition* with a hypothetical emphasis likely to be fulfilled in the future. Holding fast to our confidence or boldness is EVIDENCE that we are part of God's house, not a condition of staying in it. The danger is not that of "falling out," but of truly being in! Or as applied to those to whom this epistle was written: to revert to Judaism was to cast doubt on whether one was truly a part of God's house.

3. 3:14 (in the very context) reaffirms this interpretation (both 3:6 & 14 are third class conditional clauses). 3:14 reads, *"For we have been made"* or *"we have become partakers of Christ"*: the verb is perfect, passive, indicative* of γινομαι / ginomai indicating the permanence and enduring fact of the action. We have been made partakers and the results will abide.

   This statement is followed by what appears to be the condition but in reality is evidence of the abiding results of our having been made partakers: *"if we hold the beginning of our confidence steadfast unto the end"* (3rd class: probable or likely future condition*). Those who have partaken of Christ will be confident of Him and His finished work for them. They may lapse, but it will not be permanent.

4. Believers are made part of "God's house" solely on the basis of personal faith in Jesus Christ. Faith is imperceptible, inscrutable, as is regeneration.

Hebrews 3:7-4:16

Introduction to this Section

The author is now led to encourage the readers to rest in Christ's provision and watch-care over God's house. Since they constitute God's house; since Christ is the architect, builder and current administrator of God's house; since He functions mercifully and faithfully in that position, those who are His are to rest assuredly and confidently in His care. To separate these paragraphs from Christ's faithful and effective ministry as High Priest over God's house is to miss one of the author's key purposes. The following diagram emphasizes the author's design.

Introduction to Christ As High Priest	Admonitions & Warnings	Prayer Encouragement because of our High Priest
<u>2:17,18</u> Christ is the faithful, merciful, capable High Priest. <u>3:1-6</u> Appeal to consider Christ's faithfulness as High Priest over God's house.	<u>3:7-4:13</u> Four (4) exhortations for the Believer to rest on or have confidence in Christ's care and provision.	<u>4:14-16</u> Because we have such an High Priest, we are exhorted to come boldly to God's throne of grace with our needs.

Actually, from 2:17 through 10:21 (last mention of Christ as High Priest), Christ's faithfulness in His office of High Priest is in view and from that basic fact flow recurring encouragements and exhortations for faith or confident rest in Him (4:1,9-11,14-16; 10:22-25,35-38; 11:1- - entire chapter; 12:1,2,15).

Key Words in 3:7-4:16: "Rest," Unbelief," "Hardness of heart"

The dominant word in these paragraphs is "rest", καταπαυσιν / *katapausin*, which means "cessation of activity," "a state of settled tranquility." Παυω / pauo means "to cease or desist," and the prefixed preposition κατα / *kata* intensifies that meaning: hence καταπαυω/ *katapauō* speaks of fixed or stable trust and rest, of calm confidence, of a relaxed, yet dynamic faith. The noun form is used in 3:11, 18; 4:1, 3, 5, 8, 10, 11: the verb form in 4:4. This "rest" is spoken of as "God's rest" (3:11, 18; 4:1, 3, 10), since He provides it. God is the source of rest, His provision and Person its object.

Another key word is "unbelief" (απιστια / *apistia*) which means "lack of confidence," "absence of trust": see 3:12, 19. Compare 4:2, 3 where its antonym "belief" or "faith" (πιστις / *pistis*) is used. The wilderness generation of Israel was not permitted to enter into "His rest" (3:18), that is, into Canaan or into rest in the Promised Land in contrast to slavery in Egypt, due to their unbelief (3:19).

By combining these two key words, one can appreciate that the author is encouraging all believers to "faith rest" or "quiet confidence" in the capacities of Christ to work all things

together for their good (even wilderness experiences!). Hebrews 3:7-4:16 could be entitled "The Romans 8:28 Section of Hebrews"!

Repeated throughout is the quotation from Psalm 95:7,8 "**Today**, if you will hear His voice, harden not your heart," 3:7, 13, 15; 4:7. This recurring admonition is against stubbornness of mind that refuses to rest in the provision of God: i.e., the mind-set of unbelief.

An Outline of 3:7-4:16: Encouragement to Faith-Rest

Almost every paragraph of Hebrews 3:7-4:16 is introduced by the word "therefore" (οὖν / *oun*: 3:7; 4: 1, 11, 14, 16), so it is obvious that the author is coming to conclusions based upon preceding information. All of these conclusions are expressed in the hortatory form: they are exhortations or admonitions, which in every case encourage us to faith-rest. Therefore, the section outlines itself grammatically as follows:

I.   Exhortation against hardness (stubbornness) of heart, 3:7-11
        (As per Wilderness Generation of Israel: <u>what faith-rest is not!</u>)

II.   Exhortation to vigilance about unbelief, 3:12-19
        (Wilderness Generation's unbelief meant no rest)

III.   Exhortation about our failing to enter into faith-rest, 4:1-10

IV.   Exhortation to give diligence to enter, 4:11-13

V.   Exhortation to come to grips with our profession, 4:14-15

VI.   Exhortation to pray with confidence, 4:16

The ensuing exposition will follow this outline.

I. Exhortation against hardness (stubbornness) of heart, 3:7-11

3:7-11 *Therefore, as the Holy Spirit says: "Today, if you will hear His voice, 8 Do not harden your hearts as in the rebellion, In the day of trial in the wilderness, 9 Where your fathers tested Me, tried Me, And saw My works forty years. 10 Therefore I was angry with that generation, And said, 'They always go astray in their heart, And they have not known My ways.' 11 So I swore in My wrath, 'They shall not enter My rest.' "*

<u>A more literal translation</u>: *"Wherefore, just as the Holy Spirit is saying, 'Today if you hear the voice of Him, do not harden your hearts as (they did) when they provoked me in the day of testing in the wilderness: when your fathers tested Me and proved Me and saw My works forty years. Wherefore, I was sorely vexed with this generation and I said, 'They always are going astray in the heart and they knew not the ways of Me.' As I swore in my wrath, 'They shall not enter into My rest.'"*

A. **v.7**: ***"as the Holy Spirit <u>is saying</u>..."*** note the implications of the inspiration of Scripture in this statement (repeated in 3:13, 15, & 4:7). "Is saying" is present tense which indicates durative action: it could be translated "keeps on saying." The quote is

from Psalm 95:7-11, most likely written by David <u>and directed toward believers</u>. Psalm 95:7 reads, *"He is our God; and we are the people of His pasture, and the sheep of His land. Today if you will hear His voice, harden not ... etc."* The admonition both in Psalm 95 and Hebrews 3 is toward believers (see further proof of this in comments on 3:12).

B. **v.8**: ***"do not harden your hearts"*** translates   σκληρυνω/ *sklērunō*, "to harden," "to make firm or stubborn," hence, "to be resistant." "Heart" is the deepest resource of the mind-soul-intellect: it is used over 600 times in the Old Testament. "Heart" is well equated with one's frame of reference. To harden the heart is to stubbornly and obstinately resist the communication, message, and/or direction of the Lord in the believer's life! The wilderness generation of Israel well illustrates this stubborn resistance of which every believer is capable.

"As in the provocation" (KJV) or ***"when they provoked Me"*** (NKJV) is a very strong indictment against the wilderness generation: the word "provocation" is παρακρασμος / *parakrasmos*, "exacerbation," "exasperation," "a treating with contempt"! These Israelites (they were believers) were exasperating! The Hebrew word (Psalm 95:8) is *meribah* which means "strife," "contention," "provoking." What a mess: they were redeemed and delivered from Egypt by the mighty hand of God, only to provoke Him in the wilderness by their stubborn hearts, manifested by their bickering, complaining, negative attitudes toward God.

"In the day of testing in the wilderness" clearly identifies this as the Exodus generation episode. By application: every believer can expect a "wilderness experience" as God leads him/her through life's pilgrimage, <u>but one is not to wander in the wilderness nor harden his mind to God's wonderful and gracious provision there</u>. Faith-rest in grace provision is the name of the game <u>at all times</u> in the believer's experience. God will work all things together one's good. Believe it!

C. **v.9**: "they tempted (πειραζω / *peirazō*) Me, they proved (δοκιμαζω / *dokimazō*) Me, and they saw (ὁραω / *horaō*) My works:" all three words are constantive aorists, meaning they repeatedly tempted, proved, and saw! Regardless of God's repeated demonstrations of love and care, they hardened their minds to Him. God records His conclusion in Numbers 14:22, *"...these ten times have they tempted Me and have not hearkened to My voice: surely they will not see the land which I sware unto their fathers."* What was the hang-up of the Exodus generation? Simply that they kept demanding that God prove Himself to them (as at the waters of Marah, with the manna, over the thirst issue at Meribah, the complaining at Taberah, the desire for fleshly meat at Kibbroth-hattaavah, etc.). And despite God's magnificent display of grace provision, they audaciously and persistently accused Him of leading them into the wilderness to do them evil (cmp. Ex.16:3; 17:3; Nu. 11:1; 14:3; 20:3-5). They had trusted the Lord to save them out of the degradation of Egypt, but were very negative about His care for them in the wilderness. They refused to exercise the daily trust and confidence that the Lord rightfully deserves. <u>Faith-rest was not part of their mentality</u>.

D. **v.10,11**: <u>God's response</u>: ***"I was angry, grieved...,"*** προσοχθιζω / *prosochthizō*, "to be sorely vexed, extremely angry."

God's evaluation: *"they always go astray* (present <u>middle</u> indicative*) *in the heart* (frame of reference): *they have not known* (aorist active indicative*) *or they have not meaningfully interacted with My ways."* In choosing their ways, they rejected God's ways. Faith-rest means we rest in the fact that His ways are the best ways for our lives.

God's conclusion of the matter: *"I swore* (I took an oath*), They shall not enter into My rest."* Literally, this clause reads *"as I swore in My wrath, if they shall enter into My rest"* (same in 4:5), meaning, *"if they enter My rest, I am not God, My word or My oath is meaningless."* That generation did not make it into Canaan rest – they were strewn all over the wilderness (see 3:17-19). Think of it: corpses everywhere; over 600,000 of them. Tombstones all over the Kadesh-Barnea area! Hardness of heart, refusal to faith-rest their daily lives, rejection or negative-ness to God's provision tempted God to the limit. He Himself takes an oath that righteously debars them from entering His rest, even though He had brought them out of Egypt for that purpose. They were not lost. They were believers. They did not lose their salvation. They simply cut short their lives and missed the blessing of fulfilled promises.

Having set forth what faith-rest is not via the Exodus generation example, the author now exhorts the Hebrew Christians not to follow suit (v.12ff).

II. Exhortation to vigilance about unbelief and to mutual encouragement, 3:12-19

> **3:12-13** *Beware, brethren, lest there be in any of you an evil heart of unbelief in departing from the living God; 13 but exhort one another daily, while it is called "Today," lest any of you be hardened through the deceitfulness of sin.*

A clarifying translation: *"Be continually taking a hard look, brethren, lest there be in any one of you an evil heart of unbelief in departing from the living God. But keep on encouraging one another day by day, as long as it is called 'today,' lest any one of you be hardened through the deceitfulness of the sin."*

A. Exhortation to guard against unbelief, v.12

    1. the exhortation, v.12a

        "keep taking a hard look," "keep taking heed," "keep being on the look-out" translates βλεπω / blepo in the present active imperative* form.

        Unbelief is not only a crippler; it leads to disobedience and deeper rebellion against God (as per the Exodus generation): therefore, each believer is to mount guard against it in his/her own mind.

    2. those addressed in the exhortation: **"Brethren,"** v.12b

        <u>This word governs or is critical to the interpretation of this entire section (3:7-4:16).</u> <u>**These exhortations are for believers.**</u>

Further evidence that <u>persons falling short of salvation</u> are <u>not</u> addressed, but true believers are, can be found in:

- Heb. 4:9 where the rest spoken of in this very context is for God's people (not unbelievers)

-1Cor. 10:1-6 where the Exodus generation that perished in the Wilderness "all drank of that spiritual Rock, Christ." They were believers: they <u>did not</u> lose their salvation: they simply cut short their physical lives due to persistent carnality due to unbelief.

- Psalm 95:6-11 where those addressed as the sheep of God's pasture are exhorted not to harden their hearts as in the provocation, etc. They were believers.

That believers are the primary target for these exhortations (Heb. 3:7, 12, 13; 4:1, 11, 14, 15) is beyond question. The text decides the point.

3. the reason for the exhortation, v.12c

"lest there be in any one of you an evil heart of unbelief in departing from the living God."

Note: <u>conduct</u> is not in view: <u>attitude</u> is. Unbelief is a matter related to the heart, the deepest resource of the mind, soul, spirit, the frame of reference (observe how Paul uses the word "heart" in Romans 10:5-10).

An evil frame of reference of unbelief means departure (αποστηναι / *apostēnai*) from the <u>living God</u>, not removal from some creed or church organization. Unbelief manifests itself in disobedience since it refuses to take into account the personal dealings of the living God. Again, the Exodus generation is an example of the manifestations of unbelief in the mentality. Note that the individual believer is to examine his own heart for unbelief, whereas the encouragement (v.13) is a mutual responsibility.

B. Exhortation to mutual encouragement, v.13

1. the exhortation, v.13a

"but keep on encouraging one another day by day as long as it is called 'today'"

"day by day" means constantly. Perhaps no command in the New Testament is as ignored as this! Believers are to encourage one another persistently. Unbelief is subtle, insidious and disastrous if left to run its course. Mutual encouragement in the things of the faith helps stymie the incursions of unbelief.

2. the reason for the exhortation, v.13b

"lest any of you (the brethren) be hardened through the deceitfulness of <u>the</u> sin (of unbelief)."

"Be hardened" is aorist passive subjunctive* from σκληρυνω / *sklerunō* (see the comments on this word in 3:7). The means of deception is expressed: the <u>deceitfulness</u> of <u>the sin</u>. Most likely the article with sin is the article of previous reference referring back to <u>unbelief</u> in v.12. All sin is deceptive, but perhaps none like that of unbelief. Unbelief enslaves to human viewpoint; unbelief causes the old frame of reference to assert itself; unbelief leads to departure from the living God. And as this verse warns, unbelief hardens the mind, meaning, it decreases the believer's capacity for reception and appreciation of the truth of God.

3.   support basis for the exhortations, v.14

> **3:14 *For we have become partakers of Christ*** (the Messiah) ***if we hold the beginning of our confidence steadfast to the en***d,

<u>God has done something permanent</u>: that is, He made us partakers or sharers of the Messiah! "Partakers" is μεταχοι / *metochēoi*, "holders in common," "sharers;" it is used in 1:9; 3:1,14; 6:4; 12:10. The verb "have become" is the perfect passive indicative* of γινομαι / *ginomai*, "to be" or "to become something": the perfect tense calls attention to the abiding results of the action: the passive voice means we were acted upon by God (we did not perform the action ourselves); the indicative mode affirms the reality of the action. True believers are actual partakers of Christ in a permanent way!

<u>We will do something</u>: ***"if we hold fast our confidence, etc."*** is a 3rd class conditional clause*: it assumes that true believers would not renounce their initial confidence in Christ. This is not a condition to being a child of God: it does not assume that union with Christ depends upon holding confidence firm or fast. What it does assume is that those who have partaken of Christ will be confident of Him and His finished work for them. Believers may lapse, but lapses are not permanent because <u>what God has done is permanent</u> (see notes on 3:6, p. 38, for further comments on this same conditional clause).

v.14 is the ground for the exhortations in v.12 & 13: i.e., since we are permanent partakers of Christ, we should keep encouraging one another relative to the faith and keep personally and individually examining our hearts to weed-out unbelief.

4.   further stimulus to heed the exhortation, v.15

> **3:15 *while it is said: "Today, if you will hear His voice, Do not harden your hearts as in the rebellion."***

<u>Clarifying translation</u>: *"While it is being said (or "in the fact that it is being said"), 'Today if you hear His voice, harden not your hearts as when they provoked Me (or "as in the provocation").'"*

Israel's exacerbation of God in the wilderness is repeatedly referred to in this section to encourage all believers <u>not to follow</u> that example of stubbornness and/or callousness of mind toward the One who has redeemed them. This

statement is repeated in 3:7, 13, 15; 4:7. Its source is Psalm 95:7-11 in which the psalmist warns his generation of the same danger.

5. <u>five questions</u> to stimulate thought on this issue, v.16-18

3:16-18 *For who, having heard, rebelled? Indeed, was it not all who came out of Egypt, led by Moses? 17 Now with whom was He angry forty years? Was it not with those who sinned, whose corpses fell in the wilderness? 18 And to whom did He swear that they would not enter His rest, but to those who did not obey?*

#1: "For who when they heard provoked (Him)?" v.16a

#2: "(Was it) not all that came out of Egypt by Moses?" v.16b

"All" here means the vast majority: practically all. The fact that a majority embraces evil does not sanction it: unanimity of unbelief does not make it right or acceptable in God's sight.

#3: "And with whom was He vexed for forty years?" v.17a

#4: "(Was it) not with them that had sinned, whose bodies fell in the wilderness?" v.17b

"Sinned" sums up the collective evils: rebellion, rejection of His authority, distaste over His provision, idolatry, complaining, etc. On Israel's choices in the Wilderness, see Psalm 78:5-17, 35-41, 52-57; 81:10-12; 95:7-11; 106:7-26

#5: "And to whom did He sware that they should not enter into His rest, but to those who were disobedient?"

Nu. 14:23, 28-30 and Deut. 1:34-35 record the oath of God in this regard. Canaan there is pictured as a haven of rest for Israel as opposed to the slavery in Egypt. Of course, the overall application of the passage here (as well as there) is the fact that without faith in God's person and provision, there will be no rest for the believer. The word <u>disobedient</u> in Greek is απειθης / apeithes meaning, "one who will not be persuaded," "one who refuses belief-type-obedience." Unbelief in daily experiences resulted in disobedience: hence the Hebrew Christians are exhorted not to follow such a pattern.

6. the Author's conclusion, v.19

3:19 *So we see that they could not enter in because of unbelief.*

<u>A literal translation</u>: *"And we are seeing then, that they were not able to enter in because of unbelief."*

Unbelief is the antithesis of faith that rests! The wilderness gang serve as an illustration of what faith-rest is not; their unbelief is a warning <u>to us</u>.

Exodus Generation	Us (N.T. Believers)
- 3:8-11, 16-19	- 3:7, 12-15
- had God's promises and provisions	- have God's promises and provisions
- failed to appropriate by faith	- must not fail to appropriate these in time-experience
- result: no genuine day by day rest in God: not prevailing trust	- hence, the 6 exhortations in Hebrews 3:7-4:16
- result: much disobedience	
- result: God did not permit them to enter	

<u>Now the point simply is this</u>: are we knowledgeable of God and His relationship to the issues of our personal lives? If so, are we looking to Him (active faith) and resting in Him (faith-rest) for direction, strength, wisdom and/or provision? IF WE ARE NOT, WE AUTOMATICALLY ARE LOOKING ELSEWHERE…TO HUMAN ABILITY, HUMAN VIEWPOINT, HUMAN STRENGTH, HUMAN RESOURCES. These will fail us – even religion fails – but the personal, absolute God never fails! He did not fail the Exodus gang when they got the Red Sea jitters (Ex. 14); nor were their parched throats too great a problem for Him at Marah (Ex. 15); nor their empty stomachs in the Wilderness of Sin (Ex. 16); nor the thirst issue at Rephidim (Ex. 17) etc., etc. God is personal and dependable: He will never fail of His promises to any believer of any age. Rest in Him!

That given of Israel's history in chapter 3 is now applied in chapter 4 with emphasis on 3 facts:

(1) Israel failed to enter into rest because of unbelief;

(2) Rest is available to believers now;

(3) Believers are to be diligent to enter into this rest now.

Moreover, God has provided a perfect means of judging unbelief or whatever would keep the believer from entering into rest; that means is the Word of God, which is able to penetrate and discern the thoughts of the heart (4:12,13).

The exhortations continue (all hortatory subjunctive verbs*):

-    "Let us fear … lest any come short of rest," 4:1

-    "Let us labor (lit. "be diligent") to enter into that rest," 4:11

-    "Let us hold fast our profession," 4:14

-   "Let us come boldly unto the throne of grace," 4:16

III. Exhortation about our failing to enter into faith-rest, 4:1-10

4:1 *Therefore, since a promise remains of entering His rest, let us fear lest any of you seem to have come short of it.*

<u>Clarifying translation</u>: *"Let us therefore fear, as there is still left a promise to enter into His rest, lest any one of you should seem to have fallen short (of it)."*

A. The Exhortation, v.1a

"Let us fear, therefore fear…": since Israel, once redeemed from bondage, never entered, let's make certain the same is not true of us. Belief in Christ is a beginning, not an end of faith-rest. Make certain that day-by-day rest in the Lord is part and parcel of your thinking process. Note that the author again includes himself ("let <u>us</u> fear"). The fear is legitimate, for failing to rest means that human viewpoint has superseded Divine viewpoint in the believer's mind.

1. the Divine promise of rest remains, v.1b

" … since a promise remains of entering into His rest"

"A promise left" is the availability of rest in the perfection and completion of God's work. It was given to believers among Israel, and it still hold good for us. What God has done, is doing and will do is to be rested in. The present tense of the participle ($\kappa\alpha\tau\alpha\lambda\epsilon\iota\pi\omega\mu\epsilon\nu\eta\varsigma$ / *kataleipomenēs*) highlights its durative action and present fact. In this regard, all of God's promises are to be depended upon: they will be fulfilled. The believer must be careful to distinguish between specific promises to Israel and those for the Church. There are, of course, promises in God's Word that are for all believers of all ages. Not one will fail!

2. the potential failure, v.1c

" … anyone of you should seem to have come short (of it)."

"should seem" is aorist active subjunctive* from $\delta o\kappa\epsilon\omega$ / *dokeō*, meaning either 1) "to appear true from the viewpoint of others," hence, "to be judged true," or 2) "to appear or seem to be true to someone."

The latter is to be preferred since the emphasis is that rest <u>is really attainable now</u> regardless of what one thinks. *"To have fallen short of it"* is a perfect infinitive which supports this interpretation. The idea is that some believer may think that he has fallen short of God's rest and that this condition cannot be remedied (emphasis of the perfect tense; i.e., "fallen short" with abiding results). The continued availability of God's rest ("peace," "confidence," "quiet hope," etc.) is emphasized. That every believer enjoys that rest by faith should be a legitimate concern of all.

B. The key ingredient of this rest: faith, v.2

4:2 ***For indeed the gospel was preached to us as well as to them; but the word which they heard did not profit them, not being mixed with faith in those who heard it.***

<u>A clarifying translation</u>:   *"For indeed we have had good news preached to us* (the entire concept of rest in Christ and the Christian way of life), *just as those also, but the word they heard did not profit those because not having been mixed with faith in them that heard."*

1. the similar message: salvation by grace

    Salvation has always been by God's grace, meaning: salvation rests upon God's abilities and provisions and not upon those of men.   Man's merit is totally excluded by God's grace. This is true of all phases of salvation: <u>both justification and sanctification are by grace provision and are not by human works or merits</u>. Such is the consistent message of God's Word. The wilderness gang heard good news; it was applicable to their wilderness situation, but it did not profit them.

2. the key ingredient: faith in God's message or words

    Like cement by itself remains isolated and non-utilitarian unless mixed with water and sand, so is the message of God's faithfulness to His people. Unless mixed with personal faith it is profitless. Conversely: mix God's promises with faith and <u>great benefit follows</u>! One must bear in mind that the <u>primary application of this passage is for believers</u>.

C. The present reality of rest illustrated in Creation, v.3-5

> **4:3-5** ***For we who have believed do enter that rest, as He has said: "So I swore in My wrath, 'They shall not enter My rest,' " although the works were finished from the foundation of the world. 4 For He has spoken in a certain place of the seventh day in this way: "And God rested on the seventh day from all His works"; 5 and again in this place: "They shall not enter My rest."***

1. v.3 has a double emphasis:

    <u>First</u>, there are those who do enjoy God's rest: "for we are entering (present active indicative*) God's rest, we who believed (aorist tense participle*)," i.e., only those who exercise trust enter this rest.

    <u>Second</u>, the negative quote follows to highlight what has just been said: "Even as He has said, as I swore in my wrath, they shall not enter into my rest ...," i.e., because they refused to exercise confidence, they could not enjoy or be involved in the rest God provides.

2. v.4 illustrates the "rest" being spoken of

    "And God rested on the seventh day from all His works": He rested, not because He was tired, but because His work was complete. Every thing that was needed for mankind was finished. The almighty God deemed that nothing more need be done; therefore, He rested. He found solace and rest in the perfection and

completion of His work. And His work is the basis of the rest spoken of in this context. Our salvation in Christ is complete: it cannot be improved upon by our doings and it can only be properly applied by resting in Him.

3. v.5 reaffirms God's oath

Lit. *"If they shall enter into My rest,"* meaning, *"My name is not God if they shall enter into My rest."* Active trust in the living God is the only way to enjoy the peace and rest that He alone provides.

The vagueness of the references in the Old Testament is indicative that the author anticipated that his readers were knowledgeable in that regard.

D. The Divine promise of rest still holds good, v.6-10

4:6-7 *Since therefore it remains that some must enter it, and those to whom it was first preached did not enter because of disobedience, 7 again He designates a certain day, saying in David, "Today," after such a long time, as it has been said: "Today, if you will hear His voice, Do not harden your hearts."*

1. v.6,7 speak of failure in the past and reaffirmation (of the rest) in the present.

The logic is:

- The Exodus gang were told of God's perfect rest-provision for them which is to be entered into by faith;

- They did not enter into that rest;

- The rest still remains for God's people;

- God reaffirms that it remains by speaking of it as being present ("today") in the time of David, some 450 years after the Exodus.

The point is that long after the wilderness gang was overthrown and even after Joshua led the next generation into Canaan, God spoke of the potentialities of rest for His people. David's generation was challenged to faith-rest. Moreover, Hebrews 3:7,13,15 direct the same challenge to us.

2. v. 8 supports the logic of v.6 & 7: Joshua did not give this rest.

4:8 *For if Joshua had given them rest, then He would not afterward have spoken of another day.*

Clarifying translation: *"for if Joshua had given them rest, He (God) would not have spoken of another day after that."*

The distribution of Canaan to the twelve tribes did not fulfill all that God spoke of when He talked of rest; that is, the settlement of the twelve tribes in Canaan did not fulfill all of God's promise of rest for His people. The author is seeking to seal the fact that God's rest remains at all times for His people.

3. v.9,10 is the climax and qualification of this entire section: God's rest remains for believers: it means on the one hand an end to their confidence in human works and on the other, a rest type confidence in God's work in Christ.

> **4:9,10** ***There remains therefore a rest for the people of God.   10 For he who has entered His rest has himself also ceased from his works as God did from His.***

Clarifying translation: *"There keeps on remaining therefore, a Sabbath-type-rest for the people of God, for the one who has entered into His (God's) rest, has himself rested from his own works, just as God did from His."*

a. v.9, "a Sabbath-type-rest keeps on remaining for the people of God"

"Sabbath-type-rest" translates σαββατισμος / *sabbatismos*, a translation (plus a Greek suffix) from the Hebrew שָׁבַת / shabath, "to rest," "to cease from working." Whereas Old Testament believers observed one day of rest per week, we are now called to a continual, abiding day-by-day rest in Christ. Day observances are past; God rests eternally in the work of Christ and so should we. This verse lends added support to the fact that the rest spoken of in this context is for believers (and not for unbelievers or someone "falling short of salvation").

b. v.10 defines or qualifies the word "rest"

"The one who has entered (aorist articular participle*) *into His (God's rest) has ceased* (or "rested:" the verb is aorist active indicative* from καταπαυω / *katapauō) also from his own works."*

- Faith-rest therefore, in the context means to cease from working to please God and to trust in what Christ has provided or worked out to please Him.

- Faith-rest means we are to cease from our own doings and trust His doings.

- Faith-rest includes trust in Divine dynamics and rejection of human dynamics for the Christian way of life.

- Faith-rest means that Divine dynamics will swing into operation when the believer trusts in them.

- Faith-rest means living life from the relaxed position in Christ as opposed to ceaseless activity in the energy of the flesh.

- Faith-rest means we rest from our works as God did from His: that "rest" is to characterize the mentality of the believer throughout all of his/her Christian experience.

Summary of Faith-Rest Principles

It is time to summarize faith-rest principles before we move on to Hebrews 4:11-16.

1. Faith-rest is confidence or belief in the veracity of God, His Word, His perfect grace-provision, His promises, His teaching concerning Himself and His relation to you. There is no such thing as blind faith from God's point of view.

2. Faith-rest means the believer ceases from the working principle and relaxes in the security of God's essence and pronouncements.

3. Faith-rest requires that we know God and His promises and that we appropriate these in our personal lives.

4. Faith-rest <u>is not passivity</u> or indolence: we change what we can; we rest what we cannot change into God's hands.

5. Faith-rest <u>is never stagnant or fossilized</u>. <u>Faith is always active… in the now, hence the emphasis is on TODAY as in Hebrews 3 & 4</u> (3:7, 12, 13, 15; 4:7). The implication is that there will always be something for which the believer is to trust to or rest in the Lord.

6. Faith-rest is moment-by-moment trust in the Divine operating assets for the age in which one lives. Hence, such statements by Paul:

   - "I live by faith," Gal 2:20;

   - "We walk or conduct our lives by faith," 2Cor. 5:7;

   - "Whatsoever is not of faith is sin," Rom. 14:23

7. Faith in Christ's work at Calvary = Salvation (John 3:16; Acts 16:31).

   Faith in God's written word = Assurance, Knowledgeability (1John 5:10-14).

   Faith in "in Christ" truths = Maturation (2Peter 3:18).

8. Three Biblical illustrations of faith-rest:

   David in I Sam. 17 refused human dynamics in fighting Goliath (see 17:38,39 where he refuses Saul's armor): he knew the battle was the Lord's (17:47). He rests in Divine provision as he rushes (faith results in action) to the enemy (17:48).

   Daniel in Babylon refuses the provision of Nebuchadnezzar (Dan. 1:8), an act tantamount with treason and punishable by death. Daniel was resting in God's provision and ends up in favor in the court (1:19-21).

   Joseph before he dies in Egypt extracts an oath from the Jews that they will not let his bones rot there, but carry them to Palestine (Gen. 50:25). He rested in God's promise that He would deliver the children of Israel from the bondage of Egypt (Compare Gen. 15:13, 14; Ex. 13:19; Heb. 11:22).

IV. Exhortation to give diligence to enter that rest, 4:11-13

4:11 *Let us therefore be diligent to enter that rest, lest anyone fall according to the same example of disobedience.*

A. The exhortation, v.11a

"Let us be diligent to enter into that rest (lit. "...into that, the rest")"

The King James, "let us labor" is very confusing here, since the author has just stated that the rest he is speaking of is not characterized by work! *Let us be diligent* is a much better translation of the verb σπουδαζω / *spoudazō*, a verb that combines the ideas of eagerness, earnestness, and diligence. Speedy and active involvement, the opposites of lazy and passive attitudes, are in view. The aorist tense means, "Get with it right now!" Make certain diligence in this faith-rest matter is part and parcel of your mentality." For further uses of *spoudazo*, see 2Tim. 2:15; 4:9, 21; Eph. 4:3; 2Pet. 1:15.

This is the first of three final concluding admonitions that wind-up the second movement of this magnificent section:

- v.11, "therefore, let us be diligent to enter into that rest..."

- v.14, "therefore, let us come to grips with our profession..."

- v.16, "therefore, let us come boldly to the throne of grace..."

Note that each begins with the same summing-up word, "therefore," meaning, on the basis of some logical presentation of thought, a conclusion is about to be expressed. In each case, the conclusion is an exhortation to action: that is, what ought to be done in view of what has been said.

B. The preventative concept in the exhortation, v.11b

"Lest anyone should fall through the same example of disobedience."

God provides rest-type-blessings for His people. These are vital to day-by-day function in the faith. Believers are to enter into the blessings of that rest by faith, not by works. And it is possible for a believer "to fall" (aorist subjunctive* from πιπτω / *piptō*, "to fall" or "to fall to pieces"), so that his/her life is never characterized by the rest that God has provided. Such are Humpty Dumpty types: they fall apart or come unglued over the same issues that similarly effect unbelievers. The wilderness gang furnishes the negative example: why follow it?

C. Two reasons for this exhortation, v.12,13

1. the character of God's Word, v.12

4:12 *For the word of God is living and powerful, and sharper than any two-edged sword, piercing even to the division of soul and spirit, and of joints and marrow, and is a discerner of the thoughts and intents of the heart.*

<u>Clarifying translation</u>: *"For the Word of God (is) living and operative and sharper than any two-edged sword, even piercing as far as (the) division of soul and spirit, and of both joints and marrow, and able to judge thoughts and intentions of the heart."*

The Word of God in the context is God's revelation of Himself, His promises, His pronouncements, which offer rest to the believer. Four things are stated about God's Word:

a. <u>God's Word is alive</u> (ζων / *zoē*): lit. "is living" (present active participle*); i.e., it is intrinsically possessed of life; the opposite of dead or stagnant. This is so because God's Word is inseparable from His essence (compare Psa. 138:2; John 6:63), and since it is alive, it will accomplish what God purposes in it. It will not return unto Him void; it brings to Him the fulfillment of purpose for which it was designed (Isa. 55:11).

b. <u>God's Word is operative</u> (ενηργης /*energēs*): active, full of energy, powerful, able to get the job done. It is the resource of His operational power. The key thought in the word *energēs*, (think of our word <u>energy</u>) is that His Word still does what He said it will do. It is not outmoded nor is it inoperative. In the context, the Word of God offers rest: *energēs* means that it is able to deliver what it offers.

c. <u>God's Word is penetrating</u>: it lays bare the inmost being, cutting through the deepest recesses of one's essence. His Word penetrates and exposes the problems of the mind. The analogy to "joints and marrow" suggests the distinction between that which is extrinsic (outward, external) with that which is intrinsic (inward, internal). God's Word gets to the core of the problem: there it is alive and operative, able to perform, expose, stimulate, bring to pass His purposes. His Word is precisely what is needed relative to true faith, faith's true object, and faith's benefits.

d. <u>God's Word is a judge, a critic</u>: a κριτικος / *kritokos*. His Word "sits in judgment," "discerns," "is capable of criticism" of the unseen: the thoughts and intentions of our hearts. Involved are our aspiration and motivations. The Word of God is the real evaluator of desires, intentions, motivations. In context, it critiques these vital aspects of our heart since they relate to unbelief and belief. And it is given that we might perceive the folly of anything short of true rest in His provisions.

Other passages on the nature and capabilities of God's Word are:

- 1Peter 1:23, God's Word is the agent in regeneration;

- James 1:21, God's Word implanted delivers the soul;

- John 17:17, God's Word is the medium of sanctification;

- Acts 20:32, God's Word is the medium of edification;

- Eph. 6:17, God's Word is the chief offensive weapon of the equipped believer.

2. the character of God, v.13 (the second reason for the exhortation in v. 12-13)

4:13 *And there is no creature hidden from His sight, but all things are naked and open to the eyes of Him to Whom we must give account.*

Clarifying translation: *"And there is no created thing not manifest before Him, but all things are naked and having been laid bare to the eyes of Him, toward Whom (is) our word (or account)."*

Three things intended:

a. God sees all, even the unseen thoughts and intents of the heart.

b. God sees all clearly or truly: thoughts, emotions, acts, impulses, motivations are stripped of all pretense, veneers, artificial coverings, superficial masks. There can be no pretense or disguise with God. Nor can the true facts of any part of our being be hid from Him. The point of this and all scripture is to encourage one always to be honest before the Lord, to exercise confession where necessary, to see things as He sees them.

c. God is the One to Whom we are responsible: lit. *"to Whom (is) the word of us."* We are responsible to Him. In context, His Word is offering us His rest; now our word to Him should truly manifest where we stand in the matter. Again, honesty, self-judgment, confession, and consequent enjoyment of fellowship with Him and His provisions are in view.

Summary of exhortation #4: be diligent to enter into God's rest: use God's Word to test the true purposes of the heart, so that we do not fail to unmask unbelief.

V. Exhortation to come to grips with our profession, v.14,15 (Exhortation #5 in this series)

4:14 *Seeing then that we have a great High Priest who has passed through the heavens, Jesus the Son of God, let us hold fast our confession.*

Clarifying translation: *"Therefore, because we have a great high priest who has passed through the heavens, Jesus, the Son of God, let us lay hold of our profession."*

A. The basis of the exhortation, v.14a, the fact of Christ's priesthood.

The participle εχοντες / *echēontes* is causal, and thus is the basis of the exhortation *(because we keep on having a great high priest")*. There will never be a time in our human need that Christ, our great high priest, is not functioning in our behalf nor will He ever fail to communicate the things of the Father to us.

One must remember that the high priest was a tremendous resource figure to a Jew: the author is preparing his readers for Christ's superiority in that role (chapters 5-10 will develop this). Two key factors are highlighted in v.14:

1. the finality of His priesthood

   <u>As high priest, Christ has transcended the limits of space</u>: He is *"One who has passed through the heavens."* The finality of this act is highlighted by the perfect tense: He has passed through and the results are permanent. There with God, He ever lives to intercede in the interest of believers (7:25). Aaron passed through types; Aaron had to repeat the atoning sacrifices; Aaron had to depend upon sacrificial types: but Christ passed once and for all through the heavens into the very presence of God on the basis of His own sacrifice. He entered into rest that He might bring His people into it.

2. the person who is high priest

   - "Jesus" emphasis on His relation to humanity as in 2:9; 3:1; 10:19; 12:2, 24; 13:12.

   - "the Son of God" emphasis on His Deity as in 1:2,5-13; 3:6; 5:5, 8; 6:6; 7:3, 28; 10:29.

   These two aspects of the essence of Messiah make Him perfect for the role of high priest: He very capably represents man to God and God to man. His Divine glory does not constitute a barrier between Himself and His people.

B. The exhortation, v.14b

"Let us lay hold of our profession."

Profession is ὁμολογιαν / *homologian*, "that which we profess to believe." It is often translated "confession."

"Lay hold" or *"hold fast"* translates the present active subjunctive* of κρατεω / *krateō* (compare 3:6 and 10:23 where "hold fast" is κατεχω / *katechō*. <u>*Katecho*</u> puts more emphasis on holding on to that which we possess.). Westcott says the emphasis in <u>krateo</u> is grasping and clinging to that to which we attach ourselves. Liddell-Scott says it means "to lay hold of," "get mastery or possession of." Implied is the idea of knowing, mastering, and applying to our lives that which we profess to believe, a coming to grips with the realities of our profession. Emphasis is on intense interaction with what we say we believe. *"Let's come to grips with what we are saying we believe"* is the idea.

C. More support for response to the exhortation, v.15

4:15 *For we do not have a High Priest who cannot sympathize with our weaknesses, but was in all points tempted as we are, yet without sin.*

<u>Clarifying translation</u>: *"For we are not having a high priest who is unable to empathize with our weaknesses, but one having been tempted in all things in accord with our likeness, sin apart."*

Note three things to encourage our response:

1. Christ empathizes with us in our weaknesses.

   Sympathize (from συμπαθεω / *sumpatheō*) means "to be similarly affected," "to be compassionate," "to suffer with another." Our word <u>sympathy</u> is a direct transliteration, but <u>sympathy</u> can mean mere pity, whereas <u>empathy</u> captures more the ideas of compassion and tender-heartedness in *sumpatheō*. Jesus Christ, our high priest, empathizes with the weaknesses of our humanity: His tender compassion is aroused by our human condition and the circumstances of our trials.

2. Christ was tested like as we.

   The logic in the verse is dramatically stated: first by a double negative, "We are <u>not</u> having a high priest who is <u>not</u> able to empathize with our weaknesses," then by a strong adversative <u>but</u>. *"<u>But</u>, on the contrary, we are having One who has been tested (perfect passive participle*) in all things in accord with our likeness..."* Our high priest has been tested and the positive results abide: He need not be tested again.

   Moreover, He has experienced every form of testing. He was physically born like we (this does not discredit His conception in a virgin); He grew up as we; He labored, was weary, experienced victories, defeats, joys and sorrows as we; He underwent death, His own unique death, but nevertheless, death as we. Our Lord experienced every form of trial and affliction open to mankind. He, therefore, can say to the suffering believer, "I have been there; I know how you feel." But He can do more! He can come to the aid of His suffering sheep; see 2:18!

3. Christ was sinless in His testings.

   "Sin *apart*" translates χωρις / *chōris* meaning "separate from," "without," "<u>without</u> possessing something" as in 11:6, "<u>without</u> faith, it is impossible to please God." Our Lord was tested like as we, sin apart, i.e., without possessing sin. He had no sin nature, hence, was never negative or rebellious to God in all of His testings. He was tested in every area, yet never sinned. Thus He proves His faithfulness to God on the one hand and His capabilities to help His followers on the other. And it is his sinlessness that makes His compassion to be pure, perfect, and effective toward us.

   The information in v.15 is given to encourage us to get a grip on what we profess to believe (v.14) and also to be stimulated to pray as exhorted in v.16. In other words, v.15 provides further reason to follow the exhortation of v.14 and also provides an introduction to v.16.

VI. Exhortation to pray with confidence, v.16 (Exhortation #6 in the series)

   4:16 *Let us therefore come boldly to the throne of grace, that we may obtain mercy and find grace to help in time of need.*

   <u>A literal translation</u>: *"Let us therefore keep on coming with confidence to the throne of grace in order that we may receive mercy and may find grace for timely (or "seasonable" help."*

A. The vertical stimulus to prayer

"Therefore" sums up the vertical stimulus to prayer: because Christ on high is a capable, concerned, and compassionate High Priest, do not fail to draw near the throne of grace. There we will experience His capabilities and compassions. Moreover, grace has been enthroned, a place where favor is meted out to the undeserving.

B. The invitation to pray

"Let us keep on coming or approaching the throne of grace..." The verb is present active subjunctive* of προερχομαι / *proerchomai*, "to come before," "to draw near," "to come nigh." The grandeur of our infinite privileges in Christ is in view. Unlike Israelite believers who worshipped from afar off, we are to draw near. And to what? To very Deity Himself, the center of sovereignty and love operative toward us. It is to no symbolic mercy seat that we draw near, but to the Lord of the universe Himself. And there at the Throne of His grace (the article with grace is most likely the equivalent of a possessive pronoun), the compassion of our High Priest is experienced. What was once the throne of judgment has become the throne of grace provision! No believer should fail to avail himself/herself of this glorious privilege and Divine-operating-asset of this age!

C. The attitude encouraged in prayer.

"Come <u>boldly</u> to the throne of grace."

"Boldly" translates παρρησιας / *parrēsias* which means "freedom to speak," hence "openness," "frankness," "plainness." The genitive case is often used adverbially (as here) in the New Testament. This word combines two ideas: (1) we are to come plainly or openly to God in prayer; i.e., honestly, unambiguously, without pretence; and (2) we are to come to God boldly, with confidence, and a genuine sense of liberty. Satan would seek to distort both so as to keep us from prayer.

D. The two-fold purpose of this exhortation to prayer

1. **"that we may receive mercy (for seasonable help)"**

   Mercy extended to the believer means that God answers his/her prayers in such a way that the felt need is met.

2. **"that we may find** (ευρισκω / *eupiskō*, "discover") **grace (for seasonable help)"**

   Grace means that God helps the believer bear up positively under the felt need until the issues or needs are fully met. Often mercy and grace are combined in God's answer to specific prayer.

E. The horizontal motivation in prayer

"for seasonable help" (or timely aid")

This little prepositional phrase indicates that every believer will experience felt needs in life that should be shared with God in prayer. Philippians 4:6 encourages us to express every anxiety to the Lord in prayer. Prayer itself is an expression of felt need: in context, the testings of life in themselves involve matters that we are to share in prayer.

<u>Summary</u>: This ends the section on faith that rests (3:7-4:16)! 3:1 asks us to consider Christ in the role of high priest: 3:6-4:16 exhorts us to rest in His faithfulness as the One who faithfully and capably watches over God's house, whose house we are. Rest in His care!

Hebrews 5:1-10 Introduction to Christ as Our High Priest

Having exhorted the Hebrew Christians to make certain their faith was resting in the right object, the author now begins an extended discussion of the excellencies and values of the high priestly ministries of our Lord Jesus Christ. Except for one interruption (5:11-6:20), readers are led:

- to appreciate the permanence and quality of Christ's priesthood (Ch.7);

- to realize that He mediates a new and better covenant in that role (Ch.8);

- to know that His present ministry in God's heavenly sanctuary is the fulfillment of old covenant priestly types (Ch.9a); and,

- to more fully understand that His once-for-all sacrifice of Himself is God's sole and only efficacious answer for the sins of mankind (Ch.9-10a).

Hebrews 5:1-10, then, is an introduction to the heart of this letter. These verses deal with Christ's qualifications as a High Priest of a new order (after Melchizedek rather than that of Aaron).

I. A Six-fold Description of Old Testament High Priests, 5:1-4

5:1-4 *For every high priest taken from among men is appointed for men in things pertaining to God, that he may offer both gifts and sacrifices for sins. 2   He can have compassion on those who are ignorant and going astray, since   he himself is also subject to weakness. 3 Because of this he is required as for   the people, so also for himself, to offer sacrifices for sins. 4 And no man takes   this honor to himself, but he who is called by God, just as Aaron was.*

A. Requirement: had to be *"chosen from men or mankind,"* v.1a

The priesthood in Old Testament times was limited to male descendants of Levi (the Levites). Females were prohibited. General requirements for Levitical priests are recorded in Leviticus 10 and 21. For more specific High Priestly requirements, see Leviticus 21:10-15.

One of the purposes of the Son of God taking human flesh to Himself was to fulfill this condition: *"He was made like his brethren that he might become a merciful and faithful high priest in the things pertaining to God"* (2:17).

B. Purpose of the High Priest, v.1b

"he is appointed <u>for</u> or on behalf of men in the things toward God"

The high priest was not only <u>out from mankind</u>, he was <u>for</u> or <u>in the interest</u> of mankind (the preposition is ὑπερ / *huper*). God chose or appointed the office as a prefigure or type of Christ. It is God saying in a prefigure, *"I do have a way of approach, a plan, a means whereby mankind can approach me: <u>my</u> high priest, the one I have chosen, is appointed to function for you in the things that pertain to me. If you have problems that pertain to civil law, see a civil authority: if things pertaining to finance, see a financier: <u>but in things pertaining to Me, see my high priest!</u>"*

C. A second major purpose of the High Priest, v.1c

"that he might offer both gifts and sacrifices for (ὑπερ / *huper*, *"on behalf of"* or *"in the place of" sins*).

In occupying himself with "the things pertaining to God," a major responsibility, perhaps <u>the major responsibility</u>, of the high priest was seeing to the proper sacrifice for sins. *"Gifts"* most likely refers to general sacrifices such as the meal and fat offerings: *"Sacrifices"* would be of the blood-type such as the burnt, the peace, and the sin offerings.

Note that these were offered *"for"* or *"on behalf of"* sins: the substitutionary preposition *huper* is used, meaning, the offering itself bore the penalty that sin demanded. It took the place of the person who was guilty. Old Testament offerings could not take away sins: they merely prefigured the final and efficacious offering of Jesus Christ Himself (Heb. 10:1-10).

D. Character-trait-requirement of the High Priest, v.2

"one being able to deal compassionately with the ignorant and the errant, since he himself also is encompassed with the weakness."

High Priests were to be gentle and compassionate: their work concerned itself with people who were seeking to approach the one, true, righteous God, and since they themselves were clothed (the verb is from περικειμαι / *perikeimai*, "to be surrounded with," "to be encompassed," hence "to be clothed") with weakness, they had no right to exalt themselves due to their office. "To deal compassionately" (μετριεπαθειν / *metriepathein*) means "to mediate compassion <u>without undue severity nor careless leniency</u>." The consciousness of their own natural and moral weakness was a stimulus to so deal with the people. High Priests were not to be ivory tower types!

E. Obligation and responsibility of all high priests: make offerings for personal sins, v.3

The verb *"he is required,"* ("he ought," KJV) is very strong: οφειλω / *opheilō* which means "to be bound," "to be obligated." Because every high priest had personal weakness that led to sin, he was obligated to bring sacrifices. This is graphically illustrated on the Day of Atonement (Lev. 16) where he first offers a bullock for himself and his house, then another for Israel. In this sense, Christ is in contrast: instead of having to offer a sacrifice, He Himself becomes the sinless sacrifice upon whom God lays the sins of the world (2 Cor. 5:21; John 1:29; 1John 2:2).

F. Qualification of appointment of a high priest, v.4

"and no one takes this honor to himself, but the one being called by God, even as Aaron."

Human authority could not validly appoint a high priest: the order came from God. Note how the inspiration and authority of the Old Testament comes into play: Aaron was <u>God's choice</u>, not man's (Ex. 28:1ff; Lev. 8:1ff; Nu. 16:5; 17:5; 18:1ff).

In view of this, the author now produces evidence that Jesus has the necessary Divine calling to a priesthood that not only replaces the Aaronic order but is far superior to it. Even though Jesus was God's Son, He did not assume this priestly dignity on His own initiative: He is called of God and that calling is prophesied in the Old Testament (Psalm 110:4).

II. Christ's superior high priesthood, 5:5-10

A. Christ's (Messiah's) Divine appointment / calling to this function, v.5-6

> **5:5-6 *So also Christ did not glorify Himself to become High Priest, but it was He who said to Him: "You are My Son, Today I have begotten You." 6 As He also says in another place: "You are a priest forever according to the order of Melchizedek";***

<u>Clarifying translation</u>: *"So also the Christ (the Messiah) did not glorify himself to be made a high priest, but the One who spoke concerning him, 'You are my Son; today I have begotten you,' just as He also says in another (passage), 'You are a priest forever in accord with the order of Melchizedek.'"*

Psalm 2:7 and 110:4 are quoted in that order: both are royal, Messianic Psalms which predict the domination of Messiah over the kings of the earth as well as the Melchizedek type priesthood. It is of no little consequence that David, some four hundred years after Aaron, predicts an enduring priesthood for Messiah that is not in the Levitical lineage. Why should there be another priest of a different order? Simply because the Levitical priesthood could not get the job done due to the inherent weaknesses of the priests and the ineffectualness of the sacrifices (the entire system was temporary and preparatory for Messiah). In His plan, Messiah would fulfill the necessary role, so God has David prophesy of that reality. (The author comments further on the Melchizedek typology in 7:1-10, then delineates the reasons for the Davidic prophecy of the new order in 7:11-28).

The point of 5:5-6 is that Christ is called of God to be our High Priest. In these verses are <u>three facts that set forth the glories of His priesthood</u>:

1. <u>His essential Deity</u>, "<u>Thou art my Son</u>." By His absolute oneness with the Father, we are assured of His ability and faithfulness of consistently mediating the things of the Father to us.

2. <u>His true humanity</u>, <u>sin apart</u>, "<u>Today have I begotten you</u>" (consistently used in reference to the virgin birth). By His absolute oneness with mankind, He has perfect experiential knowledge of our needs and maximal empathy with our weaknesses. In this sense, He was "made perfect" for the role of high priest through suffering, 5:7-9. See also 4:15.

3. <u>His superior, enduring order</u>, *"a priest forever after the order of Melchizedek"* (rather than that of Aaron). The significance of the Melchizedek typology is the subject matter of Ch. 7. Suffice it to say here that by virtue of His own perfections and His enduring ministry, He exercises as High Priest a perfect and complete ministry of salvation to believers. These make Jesus Christ *"able to save to the uttermost those who come to God through Him, since He always lives to make intercession for them,"* 7:25.

B. Christ's (Messiah's) preparation as a man for this function, v.7-10

   1. Past example of dependence on the Father, v.7

> **5:7 *who, in the days of His flesh, when He had offered up prayers and supplications, with vehement cries and tears to Him who was able to save Him from death, and was heard because of His godly fear,***

"In the days of his flesh" refers to Christ's earthly life. The words *"prayers"* (δεησεις / *deēsis*, "petitions for definite needs") and *"supplications"* (ικετηριας / *hiketēpias*, "cries for aid") refer primarily to His prayers in Gethsemane and at Calvary (Mt. 26:39-44; 27:46). These were directed to *"the One able to save him <u>out from within</u>* (ἐκ / *ek*) *death."* The nature of the prayer was not to be saved or delivered from dying (this He came to do according to His own words, John 10:17,18), but to be delivered "out from within" death, that is, to be resurrected. His requests were answered because of His "godly devoutness" or "genuine piety" (ευλαβεια / *eulabeia*, "healthy reverence of Deity," "devoutedness").

   2. Past example of obedience, v.8

> 5:8 ***though He was a Son, yet He learned obedience by the things which He suffered.***

Exposure to trial and suffering manifested the perfect obedience of Christ to God the Father. Christ was not taught to obey (as we must be!); he did so instinctively. That He "learned" obedience, means that in His humanity, He progressively experienced new manifestations of obedience: this, <u>even though</u> being the sublime, eternal, uncreated, only unique Son of God!

   3. The source of salvation, v.9

> **5:9 *And having been perfected, He became the author of eternal salvation to all who obey Him,***

"And having been perfected" (aorist passive participle* from τελειοω / *teleioō*) means that Christ via the days of His flesh was completely prepared, fitted, and perfected for the execution of His functions, both as Savior and High Priest. Thus, He <u>became</u> (aorist defective middle indicative* verb from γινομαι / *ginomai*) the cause or <u>source</u> (αιτιος / *aitios*, only here in the N.T.) of eternal salvation to all who obey Him. *"Obey"* is from πειθω / *peithō which means "to persuade" or "to be persuaded": to obey Him means that one is persuaded that*

His words or His Gospel are true and to be believed. Persuasion precedes belief; in fact belief is not possible without persuasion. Christ, Himself, is the personal mediating source of our salvation: BELIEVE IT! And our salvation is eternal; that is, without end! How can anyone doubt eternal security in view of such statements!

4. <u>Divine conclusion</u>: Christ is acknowledged of God as a High Priest, v.10

5:10 ***called by God as High Priest "according to the order of Melchizedek,"***

<u>Clarifying translation</u>: *"being designated by God (as) a high priest in accord with the order of Melchizedek."*

"Being designated" translates προσαγορευτηεις / *prosagoreutēeis*, "to address," "to name, salute or greet." The Father formally ascribes the title of "High Priest" to our Lord most likely in His ascension, having been perfectly fitted for it by His earthly, obedient experience.

The order of Melchizedek is an accommodative type of Christ's priesthood which will be developed in 7:1-10. Since this subject was somewhat difficult for these Hebrew Christian readers, the author now digresses to talk of their very unhealthy spiritual state (5:11-6:20).

Chapter 5:11-6:20, which comprises the next section of this commentary, also includes the third parenthetical warning.

Overview – Hebrews 5:11-6:20,
Including the Third Parenthetical Warning to the Hebrews

The author now interrupts the development of the nature of Christ's ministry on high (he will take it up again in Ch. 7) to rebuke the Hebrew Christians for their spiritual immaturity and to warn them of the dangers of their lethargic condition. The thought flow runs as follows:

- **5:11-14** The Hebrew believers had retrogressed due to sluggardly hearing of the Word of God.

- **6:1-3** They are encouraged to move on to maturity.

- **6:4-8** They are warned (via a virtual reality stated hypothetically) of a potential worsening of their state, in their case a reversion to Levitical sacrifices which make mockery of Christ's accomplishments at Calvary and which results in an impossible situation for renewal (as long as they would persist in such sacrifices).

- **6:9-11** They are encouraged toward the kind of doctrinal diligence that produces full and lasting assurance (in what only God can accomplish).

- **6:12-15** Abraham is a good example of those who reject human abilities and trust only God to accomplish His promises.

- **6:16-18** God desires that believers, the heirs of promise, believe continually, trust perseveringly, in the immutability of His counsel. God gave two strong evidences of this counsel by two unchangeable, immutable, personal acts:

    (1) The act of making specific promise.

    (2) The act of swearing an oath by Himself.

In both cases, the believer is thrust upon the very words of Deity in order to have hope and perseverance.

- **6:19-20** This entire section properly closes with a reminder that the believer's hope is Christ, Who as our hope is:

    (1) An anchor of the soul – a stabilizer

    (2) Sure – dependable, unfailing

    (3) Steadfast – fixed, secure

    (4) The entry into the very presence of God: the Hope, the Anchor, takes hold of the very presence of God within the veil (6:19).

An Outline of 5:11-6:20

This section can be reduced to four key paragraphs (an outline by the thought-flow) that highlights the author's purposes:

I.   Rebuke for Spiritual Immaturity ("You have retrogressed"), 5:11-14

II. Exhortation for Maturation ("Let's move on to maturity"), 6:1-3

III. Virtual Reality as a Hypothetical Warning ("Your condition could worsen"), 6:4-8

IV. Confidence of the Author & Encouragement toward Full Assurance for the Readers ("We are convinced you will move on"), 6:9-20.

My exposition follows this outline.

I. Rebuke for Spiritual Immaturity ("You have retrogressed") , 5:11-14

   A. Introduction to the problems, v.11

> **5:11** *of whom we have much to say, and hard to explain, since you have become dull of hearing.*

<u>Clarifying translation</u>: *"Concerning whom, we have much to say* (lit. "much to us (is) the word") *and difficult to communicate, since you have become sluggish in hearing."*

The author wanted to say more here about Christ as high priest after the order of Melchizedek, but instead, digresses to discuss the spiritual retrogression of his Hebrew-Christian-readers. Their immaturity and mental attitudes made difficult both the communication and apprehension of Christ's priestly ministry.

     1. the communicator's problem

> ***"We have much to say"***; that is, *"there is much we want to tell you in this regard; and (it is) difficult to communicate or express."* The communicator well knew the subject matter (Christ as high priest like Melchizedek), but found the expression of it awkward <u>due to the spiritual condition of believers who were reading this letter. They should have been more mature and thus capable of handling complex subjects.</u> Imagine trying to teach third-graders the quadratic equation! Better: imagine trying to teach high school seniors interested in engineering the quadratic equation only to discover that they were having trouble figuring out what an equation is! <u>The problem was not with the communicator:</u> it was definitely with the hearers. The author well knew the spiritual condition of those who initially read this book.

     2. the hearers' problem

> ***"...since you have become dull or sluggish in hearing"***

The text literally says, *"in the hearings,"* meaning *"in the things heard."*   Ταις ακοαις / *tais akoais* can mean either: 1) the act or sense of hearing, or 2) the things heard: the second is preferable here (same in Rom. 10:16-17).

"you have become (perfect active indicative* of γινομαι / *ginomai*) *dull"* means that over a period of time, they had turned negative to the teaching of Bible doctrine and their attitudes had now crystallized into a state of spiritual lethargy and stupefaction. They had become languid (νωθρος / *nōthros*), slow, dull: the same word is translated "sluggish" in v.12 . They were not always this way: this was not a natural or inherent dullness, but one that had developed and for which they were culpable. Their dullness or lanquidness toward the teaching of the Word made the communicator's task very difficult. The author wisely considers and evaluates the condition of those with whom he seeks to communicate: true then and true now.

B. Evidence of their problem, v.12

> **5:12** *For though by this time you ought to be teachers, you need someone to teach you again the first principles of the oracles of God; and you have come to need milk and not solid food.*

<u>Clarifying translation</u>: *"For even though you ought to be teachers because of time, you keep having need* (present tense*) *for someone to teach you again the basic elements of the beginning of the oracles (the pronouncements) of God and you have become ones who keep having need* (present tense*) *of milk, not solid food."*

Dullness in the things heard, that is, in their hearing of God's Word, had taken its toll. The author now describes their condition: 1) they should have been teachers; 2) they had need to be taught the basics; and 3) they could only digest the simplest truths. The evidence against them is threefold:

1. their time without progress

   "...even though you ought to be teachers because of time"

   The Hebrew believers were exposed to good teaching; they had had time to grow; they should have grown, but they did not. In fact, they retrogressed! Growth truths bounced off their dull ears. Considering the time they had been believers, they should have been teachers; but in actuality, they needed to be taught very basic material. Instead of ministering, they needed ministering to. Spiritual lethargy is not something unique to our age.

2. their current need

   "...you keep having need that one teach you <u>again</u> the basic elements of the beginning of the oracles (the pronouncements) of God".

   "Having" is present active indicative*, meaning their need went on-and-on. That all believers need to be taught is not the issue: the problem here was the <u>continual need for basics.</u> Having to feed babies pabulum is one thing, but adults! Parents

of teenagers would be more than concerned if their children insisted on mashed carrots and peas, baby food style; yet many believers insist that communicators parrot basics ninety per cent of the time as mainline diet. In many evangelical churches, John 3:16 is served fifty-two different ways annually as a Sunday morning "meal."

"The oracles" translates the genitive plural of το λογιον / *to logion*, "the sayings," "the utterances," "the pronouncements" of Deity. Early Christians and believers today are alike in their belief that God has directed His self-revelation to mankind verbally; that Jesus Christ Himself is the climax of that self-revelation; and that that self-revelation is accurately and authoritatively recorded in Scripture. God's revelation of Himself is summed up in the expression "the oracles of God;" see Acts 7:38; Rom. 3:2; Heb. 5:12; and I Pet. 4:11 for its four uses in the New Testament. In every instance, it refers to God's utterances or communication to mankind. In context in Hebrews, the oracles are delineated as *"elementary principles"* or *"basics"* in v.12, *"the word of righteousness"* in v.13, and *"the beginning or elementary word about Messiah"* in 6:1.

3. their present condition (babyish)

"...and you have become ones who keep having need of milk, not solid food."

"Become" is perfect tense* of γινομαι / *ginomai* indicating at least two things: 1) there was a change in their essential essence: retrogression to spiritual immaturity; and 2) their babyish condition had crystallized so as to have an abiding affect upon them. <u>Think of it: it is possible for a believer to retrogress;</u> *ginomai* is used in its normal sense of "coming into a new state of existence" or "a change in essential essence." <u>They had been more mature than they were at the moment. They had become immature!</u> Back to the bottle for them; back to changing diapers for their leaders! And back to basics for everyone. *"You ought to be teachers, but you have become babes,"* says the author.

C. Confirmation of the evidence (contrast of babes and mature believers), v.13,14

5:13-14 *For everyone who partakes only of milk is unskilled in the word of righteousness, for he is a babe. 14 But solid food belongs to those who are of full age, that is, those who by reason of use have their senses exercised to discern both good and evil.*

<u>Clarifying translation</u>: *"For everyone who keeps partaking of milk is without experience of the word of righteousness: for he is a babe. But solid food is for mature ones, for ones who because of habit of mind have their faculties trained toward discernment of both good and evil."*

1. the babe, v.13

- <u>his/her staple</u> is "milk," meaning very simple, surface truths of Christianity.

- <u>his/her extension outwardly to others</u> is limited for he/she is without experience or skill (απειρος /*apeiros*) in the communication or word of righteousness. Doctrines pertaining to the word of righteousness include justification, propitiation, sanctification, and identification/positional truth. The "babe" is unskillful in these areas. Being a Christian for "x" number of years <u>does not</u> insure maturation and/or communication skills; i.e., skills in the things of the Lord. <u>M</u>aturation requires <u>k</u>nowledge <u>of</u> <u>t</u>ruth plus <u>a</u>pplication <u>of</u> <u>t</u>ruth, both of which require <u>t</u>ime (M = T + KOT + AOT). Time and proper identification with growth truth is absolutely necessary for maturation, and maturation is essential for good communication and extension of the key doctrines of Christianity.

- <u>his/her character or nature</u> is babyish: *"babe"* translates νηπιος / *nēpios*, "a non-speaking infant:" here, "an immature, childish believer." In contrast is the mature believer spoken of in v.14.

2. the mature believer, v.14

- <u>his/her staple</u> is solid food (KJV, "strong meat"). In context, "solid food" refers to doctrines that pertain to righteousness, the Melchizedek nature of Christ's priesthood, and issues relative to active faith. The mature believer grows and thrives on solid diet of Biblical truth and meaty doctrine.

- <u>his/her character or nature</u> is adultish, mature, or full age: τελειον / *teleion* means "ones who are complete," "ones who have reached the goal," in this case, the goal of Divine design: maturation in Christ.

- <u>his/her habit of mind</u> is in contrast to the <u>*nōthros*</u> (dull, lethargic) condition of these babes. *"Habit of mind"* (NKJV *"by reason of use"*) is used only here in N.T. It describes the result of the exercising of one's faculties toward discernment or judgment of good and evil. What better way of saying, ***"The mature believer keeps exercising and training his mental-spiritual faculties toward applying the word of righteousness to real life situations so he/she can discern good and evil, AND THIS IS OR BECOMES A HABIT OF MIND."***

One manifestation of maturity is the development of this critical faculty or capacity to discern what is good or evil regardless of the circumstance. The good and evil may relate to practice, to teachings, to morals, to fads, etc.

In contrast: these sluggish believers in the slough of retrogression were in danger of returning to the sacrificial system of Judaism. Such would make mockery of the death of Messiah for their sins, the very basis of their salvation; hence, the severe warning of 6:4-12.

Summary of 5:11-14 and Introduction to 6:1-3

THIS PARAGRAPH IS VERY IMPORTANT TO ONE'S UNDERSTANDING OF THE ENTIRE BOOK OF HEBREWS. It contains a general description of the Hebrew

believers who were the initial readers of this Book. It is a rebuke of their immaturity.

- v.11, they were in a state of dullness and passivity regarding Divine truth;

- v.12, they had retrogressed to *nēpios*-types (babes);

- v.13, *nēpios*-types need to be re-taught basic truths, fundamentals;

- v.14, *nēpios*-types have more difficulties with mental attitudes and discernment than do mature ones;

- 6:1-3, *nēpios*-types need to move on to maturity

II. Exhortation for Maturation ("Let's move on to maturity"), 6:1-3

6:1-3 *Therefore, leaving the discussion of the elementary principles of Christ, let us go on to perfection, not laying again the foundation of repentance from dead works and of faith toward God, 2 of the doctrine of baptisms, of laying on of hands, of resurrection of the dead, and of eternal judgment. 3 And this we will do if God permits.*

Having rebuked the Hebrew Christians for their spiritual retrogression, the author now exhorts them to move on to maturity. <u>The exhortation involves three things</u>.

A. **It involves** *"leaving the word* (or *"doctrine")* *of the beginning* (things) *of Christ* (Messiah):" that is, moving on from elementary aspects of Messiah as taught in the Old Testament.

B. **It involves** *"moving on to maturation."* The verb *"moving on"* (φερωμεθα / *pherometha*) is present <u>middle</u> subjunctive.* The middle voice requires their personal, intensive interest in moving on. *Maturation* translates τελειοτητα / *teleiotēta*, indicating "full growth" or "completion," and is often translated *perfection.* The exhortation encourages these slothful believers to give heed to God's revealed Word and move on from their babyishness to maturity.

C. **It involves** *"<u>not</u> laying down <u>again</u> the foundational* (or *basic*) *truths,"* six of which are mentioned:

- *"of repentance from dead works"*

  In essence, "You should not have to be taught again that dead works, such as Levitical sacrifices (Heb. 9:13-14), need be repented of."

- *"of faith toward God"*

  "Do we have to keep reminding you to Whom and to whose Word your faith should be directed?"

- *"of the doctrine (teachings) of baptisms"*

  "Ceremonial washings, cleansing rites and rituals related to removal of defilement in the Old Testament system are gone. Since Christ died, these are dead works." Ex. 30:19-21; Lev. 16:4,24

- *"of the laying on of hands"*

  "The identity and significance of the offerer with the offering by laying of one's hands upon its head as it was slain was foundational and need not be re-taught." Lev. 1:4; 3:2; 16:21

- *"of resurrection of dead persons"*

  "That the dead will be raised is clearly an Old Testament teaching that needs not be continually re-taught." Job 19:25-27; Psa. 17:15; Dan. 12:2; Isa. 26:19.

- ***"and of eternal punishment"***

  "Anyone who knows the Old Testament should not have to be continually reminded of eternal retribution for evil." Isa. 23:22; 66:24.

  Our author has listed six truths that he considered ABC's of the Old Testament. ABC's are foundational for elementary students, non-mature ones. They are not to be repeated in advanced grades, rather put to use expressing thought and cognitive skills: so with the basic elements of the doctrine of Messiah. Having established the basis of repentance from dead words, it is not to be re-established.

  "Let us move on to perfection / maturity," the author encourages his Jewish - Christian readers: likewise with us. Pastor-teachers should not always have to repeat basics! But to those who know not scripture and its basics, repetition is necessary.

III. Warning: A Virtual Reality Stated Somewhat Hypothetically, 6:4-8

6:4-5 *For it is impossible for those who were once enlightened, and have tasted the heavenly gift, and have become partakers of the Holy Spirit, 5 and have tasted the good word of God and the powers of the age to come, 6 if they fall away, to renew them again to repentance, since they crucify again for themselves the Son of God, and put Him to an open shame.*

This passage has suffered countless interpretations and misunderstandings throughout the history of the church, none of which will I consider here (some are considered in Addendum B).

How does one explain the Greek grammar of this text so that readers of the English text understand, comprehend, and come to a proper conclusion of its meaning? Here goes.

Explaining the Grammar of Hebrews 6:4-6 & Its Significance

First, note the connective **"for."** **"For"** connects us with the argument or logic that precedes and, in this case, the warning that follows. Preceding argument: the Jewish-Christian readers had retrogressed spiritually due to their dull, slothful attitude toward God's Word and the faith-way of the Christian life (5:11). They were babes when they should have been teachers (5:12-14). They are exhorted to move on to maturity (6:1-3). Now a stern warning introduced by the adverbial conjunction "for" (meaning "because" or "since"): *"for or since it is not possible to renew again to repentance...those* or *"the ones"* described by five participial phrases. The warning concerns itself with a certain segment persons who could not be renewed again repentance-wise. Just who are these people?

Secondly: five participial phrases describe the persons in view. Precisely WHO is critical. Let the text decide.

1. Participle #1: "those or the ones once <u>enlightened</u>..." In 10:32, this same participle is used of the Jewish <u>believers</u> to whom this book was written! It is articular (hence is adjectival in emphasis) and is in the passive voice: meaning, they were enlightened by an outward source, in this case, the Holy Spirit. Moreover, the word translated *once* (απαξ) denotes finality; i.e., enlightened once for all, not requiring repetition: it is so used in 10:2 and in 9:28 where it tells of

Christ's once for all, not to be repeated sacrifice (see also Jude :3 for the finality of this adverb). "Those once enlightened" in this context are true believers.

2. Participle #2 "and <u>have tasted</u> of the heavenly gift…" Those who advocate that unbelievers are being described say, "They tasted, but did not swallow." Apply that to 2:9 where the same verb says that Jesus tasted death for all men! Did he really enter fully into death or did he just sample it and spit it out! These tasted, swallowed, and digested the heavenly gift, just as Jesus with death. "The heavenly gift" could be none other than the Lord Jesus Christ. This participle like the others is describing true believers.

3. Participle #3 "and <u>have become</u> partakers of the Holy Spirit…" In 3:1, the recipients of this letter are called "Holy Brethren, <u>PARTAKERS</u> of the heavenly calling"; then in 3:14 "…<u>PARTAKERS</u> of Christ". All true believers are said to be <u>PARTAKERS</u> of chastisement that they might be <u>PARTAKERS</u> of His holiness in 10:8 and 10:10. "<u>PARTAKERS</u> of the Holy Spirit" can only describe true believers here and elsewhere in *Hebrews*.

4. Participle #4 "and <u>have tasted</u> the good word of God and the powers of the age to come…" "Tasted" as in Participle 2. These tasted, swallowed and digested the good word of God and the dynamic powers of the future age (the Millennium). Such statements could only describe born-again believers.

5. Participle #5 "and <u>if</u> ("and then", some translations) **<u>falling away</u>…"** Major English translations interpret this participle as adverbial/condition, hence "if" (KJV, NKJV, RSV, NIV, Amplified V). Some scholars see it as adjectival, simply following in order the other four, hence "the ones once enlightened, and tasting of the heavenly gift, … and falling away" (Darby translation, KJII, Berkeley) or "…and <u>then</u> falling away" (NASV, ASV, NRV).

Verse 6: *"if"* or *"then falling away"*: Does it Matter?

As I have pointed out, translators of the King James Version and the NKJV, RSV, and NIV, translate the fifth participle **"and <u>*IF*</u> *falling away*…"** This makes the warning conditional and thus hypothetical. I cite this only to show that a number of scholars past and present so view the passage.

Others see all five participles governed by the article that precedes only the first, in which case all five are to be understood as adjectival in force.[1] Thus the NASV, the ASV, and the NRV translations read ***"and <u>THEN</u> falling away…"***

Please note: All five describe essential qualifications of the entire group that the author has in mind. So regardless how one translates the fifth (*"then"* or *"if"*), the first four actions must precede the fifth! This means that the entire scenario is conditional: it depends upon the fulfillment of the fifth participial action and the fifth action must follow that of the first four. That an *"if"* translation is conditional is obvious; but a *"then"* translation is a less obvious condition, nevertheless real. The *"then"* description must happen after the first four. It is for this reason that I term this scenario (6:4-8) *Virtual Reality Stated Somewhat Hypothetically.*

---

[1] Daniel Wallace sees all five participles approximating a Granville Sharp plural construction: "…παραπεσαντας should be taken as adjectival, thus making a further and essential qualification of the entire group," p. 633, *Grammar Beyond the Basics*, Zondervan, 1996.

Back to our grammatical explanation: having examined the adverbial connective "for" and the five participles that describe just who is in view, we must now look at WHAT is in view. What is meant by *"falling away?"*

What is meant by *"falling away?"*

Thirdly: the segment of believers in focus are hypothetically said to have *fallen away*. Most commentators perceive this as an irrecoverable apostasy. But the participle is παραπεσοντας/ parapesontas, a second aorist from the verb παραπιπτω/ *parapiptō* (uscd only here in the New Testament). Thayer and others define *parapipto,* "to fall beside," "to slip aside," "to deviate from the right path," "to turn aside," "to wander."[1] To understand this verb or verbal as describing an irrecoverable apostasy is to stretch its essential meaning. The believers described here were in danger of serious error, deviation from the right path, of slipping aside from the basics of Christianity. But they had not apostatized. It is possible for a believer to fall away from grace-provision, but it is impossible for a believer to fall out of grace.

Precisely how does the text describe their potential error? Read on.

Fourthly: The text tells us the nature of the potential error: "(it is) impossible to renew them unto repentance…if having erred or fallen away, *since they crucify again for* (or *to*) *themselves the Son of God, and put Him to open shame.*

Just what was imminent (virtual reality) with these so described? A re-crucifixion of the Son of God! But note: a re-crucifixion **to themselves**, since it is obviously impossible for Christ in reality to be re-crucified. Also: such would put Him to open shame. How, in what manner?

The answer lies in the nature of their potential " falling aside," "their deviation from the right path," "their error," their *parapipto. Hebrews* was written to clarify the once-for-all value of the death of Messiah for the remission of sins. It is Messiah's death and His death alone that God the Father sees as efficacious where sin is the concern. Christ's singular sacrificial death is contrasted with the many sacrifices of the Levitical Covenant, which were totally ineffectual. They could never take away sin. Moreover, His sacrifice is of such value to the God the Father that it never needs repetition: it is once and for all time. This is the thrust of Hebrews 10:1-14. The author tells us twice: *"There remains no more sacrifice for sin,"* 10:18 & 26.

Therefore, for a Jewish believer to return to Temple sacrifice(s) would be the equivalent to denying the value of the once-for-all death of Messiah. It would put Messiah, the Son Of God, to open shame, and, as in 10:29, to *"tread under foot the Son of God, and count the blood of the covenant wherewith he was sanctified a common thing, and do despite to the Spirit of grace."*

Under duress from their peers, their countrymen, their families, these Hebrew Christians were tempted to revert to Temple sacrifices. To do so would be to *parapipto*, to turn aside from the most basic Christian truth! Such could only be committed while Temple sacrifices were operative. These ceased in AD 70 at the destruction of Jerusalem by the Romans. <u>No believer since could commit such an atrocious sin.</u>

---

[1] Thayer, Joseph Henry. *Greek-English Lexicon of the New Testament*, Zondervan, Grand Rapids, 1962 printing, p. 485.

Impossible Renewal unto Repentance: Meaning?

Were these believers to fulfill these conditions, their present regressive state would worsen. Already "dull of hearing," they are confronted with the seriousness of being "unable to be renewed <u>again</u> unto repentance." Having previously repented from dead works (6:1) such as Levitical sacrifices, they would have great difficulty repenting again were they to return to such worthless works! Such a condition warranted severe discipline, thus the allusion in verses 7-8 taken from the agrarian culture in which they were raised. Divine discipline is always corrective.

An Agrarian Illustration: Severe Discipline may be Ahead

6:7-8 *For the earth which drinks in the rain that often comes upon it, and bears herbs useful for those by whom it is cultivated, receives blessing from God; 8 but if it bears thorns and briars, it is rejected and near to being cursed, whose end is to be burned.*

In 6:4-6, the author issued a stern warning to shock his lethargic readers out of their dullness and retrogressive state lest it get worse. He does not accuse them of the *parapipto* described, he simply implies its possibility (virtual reality) and its consequence.

Now he follows with a simple farming illustration. Having cultivated and planted, the farmer expects the earth to bear fruit. But if it bears worthless thorns and briars, his only recourse is to burn them. Note: the farmer burns the thorns and briars, not the earth, rather what it produced!

So with the Father and His children, those begotten of Him through the new birth: like the earth, believers are cultivated and prepared by the Holy Spirit to bring forth spiritual fruit (as per John 15 and Gals. 5:22-23). But it is possible for believers to retrogress to a point of worthlessness and <u>negative production. What they produce is only worthy of fire.</u> This does not mean that such lose their salvation; they simply put themselves in danger of severe discipline. The Apostle John tells us that believers can commit a sin unto physical death, 1John 5:16. Some Corinthian believers had actually committed it, 1Cor. 11:30. They lost their rewards, not their salvation, 1Cor. 3:15.

This warning with its agrarian application is intended to grab the jugular vein of the readers and snap them out of their lethargy.

Textual Reasons Why 6:4-8 is A Virtual Reality Stated Somewhat Hypothetically

1) As already discussed, some texts, by translating the fifth participle "<u>if</u> falling away," emphasize the condition for the hypothesis to be realized. Other texts, by translating it "and <u>then</u> have fallen away," soften the hypothesis, but do not totally exclude it, since the first four positive participial phrases have to be followed by the fifth, which is negative. The negative description follows the positive and has to happen in that order. This, too, means that the situation described is conditional, hence somewhat hypothetical.

2) The shift in the subjects in view: from "we", "us", "you" in 5:11-6:3 to "they," "the ones having once-for-all being enlightened, having tasted, etc." in 6:4-6. The author is describing a circumstance unique to these thus described. It has not happened, but it could.

3) The author's own statement in verse 9: *"But, Beloved, we are persuaded better things of you, things that accompany salvation, <u>THOUGH WE THUS SPEAK</u>."* In other words, "I am not

speaking as though you have committed such a terrible error: I am merely presenting a scenario which is a virtual reality for you believers who revert to Temple sacrifices." The Hebrew Christians were to take confidence that God would complete that which He had begun in them, things that accompany salvation. But their lethargic hearing of the Word of God is not to be tolerated. Retrogression, characterized by babyishness rather than maturity, can only be corrected by positive, ongoing, faith responses to God's promises and doctrines as recorded in His Word.

IV. Confidence of the Author & Encouragement toward Full Assurance for the Readers ("We are convinced you will move on"), 6:9-20

A. The writer's confidence, v.9-10

6:9-10 *But, beloved, we are confident of better things concerning you, yes, things that accompany salvation, though we speak in this manner. 10 For God is not unjust to forget your work and labor of love which you have shown toward His name, in that you have ministered to the saints, and do minister.*

The writer states his settled conclusion: he is convinced these Hebrew Christian readers will not "fall away" from the basics they have believed. "We <u>are</u> <u>confident</u>" is a perfect passive indicative verb* from πειθω / *peitho* which means "conviction or persuasion based upon reliable evidence."

Things that accompany salvation mean truths that accompany salvation in Phases 1 and 2 (Phase 1: justification by faith alone in Christ alone; Phase 2: sanctification of the believer in time).

V.10 reaffirms the righteousness of God. He <u>will not forget</u> the good works and ministries of believers! To do so would make Him unjust, unrighteous. Note that works approved of God spring out of <u>LOVE</u>. Love of God, love of Christ, love of fellow-believers, motivate one to produce good works.

B. The writer's appeal, v. 11-12

6:11-12 *And we desire that each one of you show the same diligence to the full assurance of hope until the end, 12 that you do not become sluggish, but imitate those who through faith and patience inherit the promises.*

The writer now appeals for the same type of diligence as manifested in their service to saints (believers) be applied to <u>full</u> <u>assurance</u> of the hope presented in God's Word and promises.

Diligence translates σπουδη / *spoude*, a word that combines eagerness, readiness, zeal, effort, stick-to-itiveness. See 2 Tim. 2:16 for the verb form translated "be diligent to show yourself approved unto God, a workman…"

Full assurance (πληροφοριαν / *plērophorian*) has the definite article as does the word hope. It is <u>the</u> full assurance of <u>the</u> hope that the author highlights. What does he have in mind? Simply, absolute confidence in what God has spoken and promised! He wants these believers to move-on in Phase 2 to full assurance. Stated another way: <u>God does</u>

not want believers to doubt Him. As a believer, you should have categorical assurance of your salvation in any of its phases presented in Scripture.

Such diligence would produce <u>two</u> <u>results</u>:

1. result #1: they would not become <u>totally</u> sluggish (νωθρος / *nōthros*) in spiritual things. 5:11 told us that they had become *nōthros*: this verse implies this dullness could intensify or get worse. Diligence toward full assurance of the hope would halt the process.

   Students of the Greek text should note the grammatical formula for result here, i.e., Ίνα plus the subjunctive translated *show diligence...that you do not become sluggish*.

2. result #2: they would become imitators of the ones who in the past became recipients of promises through faith and patience.

   In order to keep from becoming total sluggards, they are to imitate those who inherit the promises through faith and patience. The major emphasis of verses 13-20 is the assurance that the saved have because of God's person (essence), promise, and oath.

C. Abraham: an example of diligence in faith and patience, v.13-15

6:13-15 *For when God made a promise to Abraham, because He could swear by no one greater, He swore by Himself, 14 saying, "Surely blessing I will bless you, and multiplying I will multiply you." 15 And so, after he had patiently endured, he obtained the promise.*

These verses are written to emphasize the grace of God. Faith (*pistis*) and patience (*makrothumia*) are fruit of the Spirit (see Gal. 5:23); in other words, one who walks in and by the Spirit will experience the fruit. The opposite of this is "walking in the flesh," in which, one produces the works of the flesh (Gal. 5:19-21).

1. v. 13 would better read "*After God made the promise to Abraham...He swore an oath.*" The question of the <u>when</u> of the oath is important – see Gen. 22:16,17 for the answer – it was years and years after the original promise was given (Gen. 12:1-3 & 15:5). Many times in between, Abraham walked in the energy of his flesh (Gen. 12:10-16; 16:1-6); but through his defeats, his faith in Jehovah grew and grew until he renounced the flesh as a means of spirituality. Proof of this lies in his willingness to sacrifice Isaac, his only son (Gen. 22:1-15: compare Heb. 11:19 where we are told that Abraham believed God would resurrect Isaac to fulfill the promise!).

   After this incident with Isaac, God interposes an oath. The promise would have been realized without the oath; the oath was added only to reassure Abraham (and us!).

2. v.13, "*He could sware by none greater*" – no one or thing is greater than God – no idea is greater than He! This is God's commentary on Himself.

3. v.14 is a powerful Hebraism, a quote of Gen. 22:16-17. The same promise was given earlier in Genesis (15:5), but reaffirmed in Ch. 22 after the sacrifice of Isaac.

4. v. 15: by the time of the Isaac-offering experience, Abraham had come to full assurance of hope (cmp. V.11,12); no more testings are recorded in the O.T. Abraham, then, becomes an example of walking in the Spirit which produces faith-patience.

D. Believers, spiritual heirs, have <u>HOPE</u> in God's unchangeable purpose, v.16-18

6:16-18 *For men indeed swear by the greater, and an oath for confirmation is for them an end of all dispute. 17 Thus God, determining to show more abundantly to the heirs of promise the immutability of His counsel, confirmed it by an oath, 18 that by two immutable things, in which it is impossible for God to lie, we might have strong consolation, who have fled for refuge to lay hold of the hope set before us.*

1. v.16: men sware oaths or sign contracts as assurance to each other. Think of your purchase contract for a home or car.

2. v.17: God, to show believers that His purposes and promises are unchangeable, *SWORE AN OATH*!

   NKJV reads, *"determining to show more abundantly to the heirs of salvation:"* KJV reads, *"willing to show more abundantly..."* The causal participle here is present tense* of βουλωμαι / *boulomai*, "desire based upon reason:" God powerfully desires that believers perceive that <u>His promises are unchangeable</u>.

   Note: God disregards the insult implied in man's doubting His word: He condescends to human infirmity by confirming His Word by an oath. <u>He is surely the God of all grace</u>!

3. v.17 *unchangeable*, αμεταθετον / *ametatheton*, fixed, unalterable, constant, stable. God will not change His position; having made a promise, He will keep it. Men sign contracts, make oaths, etc., and often violate them. NOT THE GOD OF THE BIBLE!

4. v.17 "the immutability, unchangeableness, of His <u>counsel</u>:" *counsel*, βουλη / *boulē*, means "purpose" or "will". God's counsel or purpose is unchangeable. The counsel or will expressed here are His promises of spiritual blessing to Abraham and his heirs.

5. V.18 "by two immutable <u>things</u>", πραγματα / *pragmata*, meaning "things done", "acts", "transactions." The two immutable things in context are:
   (1) the act of God making promise; and
   (2) the act of God in swearing an oath.

God's promises will never change, much less fail! His promise of salvation should be enough, but God condescends to mediate between Himself and us, swearing by His own Person to keep His promise. He first promised, then swore an oath to keep His promise!

6. v.18 – The purpose of these two immutable acts of God is that *"we might have"* (present active subjunctive*) *strong encouragement"* who have fled for refuge to lay hold of the hope (Lord Jesus Christ) set before us.

E. Jesus Christ is the "set-near hope" of the believer, v.19-20

6:19-20 *This* hope *we have as an anchor of the soul, both sure and steadfast, and which enters the Presence* behind *the veil, 20 where the forerunner has entered for us,* even *Jesus, having become High Priest forever according to the order of Melchizedek.*

1. "Set before" in v.18 could be translated "placed near," or "lying near;" that is, a hope not far removed from us. In vs. 19, 20, this "hope" is personified as "entering within the veil," that is, into the very presence of God in our behalf.

The *hope* here is:

- What Jesus Christ is.

- What Jesus Christ has accomplished.

- What Jesus Christ is doing.

- What Jesus Christ will do.

2. v.19 Four things are stated about our Hope. It is:

- **an anchor** – as an anchor secures a vessel in a tempestuous sea, so our hope, the Lord Jesus, stabilizes us in our times of trial and difficulty.

- **sure** - ασφαλης / *asphalēs* = "not liable to fall," hence "unfailing," "not betraying confidence." No one who has ever put his confidence in Jesus Christ will ever be disappointed or put to shame over it. This is the meaning of Rom. 10:11, "whosoever believes in Him shall not be put to shame."

- **steadfast** - βεβαιος / *bebaios* = "something that does not break down when put to the test," hence, "firm" or "fixed". Cmp. 2:2; 3:14.

- **entering** (present participle*) **inside the veil** = continually in the very presence of the Shekinah Glory of God on our behalf!

3. v.20 Jesus, our HOPE, is the One who goes before that He might lead us, His sheep, into God's very presence. The O.T. high priest was only a representative; he could never measure up to Christ's high priestly ministry.

Summary, Chapter 6

The author wanted to go on with the subject of Christ as High Priest after the order of Melchizedek (5:1-10), but he digressed in Chapter 5 and 6...

- to rebuke the readers for their sluggish mentality toward God's Word, **5:11-14**;

- to encourage them to go on to maturity, **6:1-3**;

- to warn them of a potential worsening of their retrogression, **6:4-8**;

- to express his confidence that they would move on, **6:9-12**;

- to reassure them of the inviobility of God's promises, **6:13-18**;

- to anchor them in Jesus Christ, Our Hope who serves within the veil, that is, Christ ministering to us in the very presence of God as our High Priest in accord with the order of Melchizedek, **6:19-20**.

He, the author, is back to the subject introduced in 5:10, Christ as our High Priest.

Chapter 7 will demonstrate the superior ministry of Christ in this role over Aaron and any that preceded Him.

Chapter 8 clarifies the superiority of a new covenant mediated by Christ to that of the old.

Chapter 9 contrasts the ministries of types and shadows under the Old Covenant with those of Christ under a new covenant.

Chapter 10 clearly states that sacrifices under the old covenant could never take away sin, but the one sacrifice of Christ, the Messiah, efficiently and solely cares for every sin of all time!

-To be continued in Volume II-

The "Greek Ready References" that follow <u>are not</u> intended for those who have only a superficial knowledge of *koine* Greek. Rather, they are to serve as reminders to those with formal and/or personal training in the grammatical functions of the language. Students are encouraged to seek further clarification in a good grammatical text. I recommend using as a handbook, Daniel W. Wallace's *Greek Grammar Beyond the Basics: An Exegetical Syntax of the New Testament*, Zondervan, Grand Rapids, 1996.

-Ron Merryman

Greek Ready Reference#1: Greek Verbs & Verbals

Verbs are action words. Verbals are either infinitives or participles. An infinitive is a verbal noun; e.g., it has qualities both of a verb and of a noun. A participle is a verbal adjective; e.g., it has qualities both of a verb and of an adjective.

All verbs have tense, voice, mode, person, & number.

Verbals have tense, voice, number, case, & usage (see Ready Refs. on Infinitives & Participles).

I. TENSE: the action-quality of the verb, both kind & time of action (emphasis is on the kind of action).

    1. <u>Present</u> tense - generally durative action in present time.
    2. <u>Imperfect</u> tense - generally durative action in past time.
    3. <u>Future</u> tense - action that will occur in future time.
    4. <u>Aorist</u> tense- the fact of the action is paramount, hence looked upon as past point fact (punctiliar); the aorist describes an event as a single whole without regarding the time taken in its accomplishment.
    5. <u>Perfect </u> tense- completed action with an emphasis on the abiding results of the action (results which abide in the present).
    6. <u>Pluperfect</u> tense- completed action with an emphasis on the abiding results in past time.

II. VOICE: quality of the verb that shows the relation of the subject to the action of the verb.

    1. <u>Active</u> voice – subject produces the action of the verb.
    2. <u>Middle</u> voice– subject is intensely involved in the results of the action; emphasis is more on the subject's involvement than on the action.
    3. <u>Passive</u> voice – subject receives the action of the verb.

III. MODE (or MOOD): shows the relation of the verb to reality.

    1. Indicative mode – action that is real or actual: mode of reality.
    2. Subjunctive mode – action that is objectively possible: mode of probability.
    3. Imperative mode – action that is volitionally possible: mode of command.
    4. Optative mode – action that is subjectively possible, but not probable: mode of improbability.

The FORM (spelling) of the verb generally tells us its tense, voice and mode.

Greek Ready Reference #2: Uses of the Infinitive in Koine Greek

I. General

The infinitive is a verbal noun.
- As a verb, it has tense and voice and may have a subject and an object, both of which are in the accusative case; the nominative case is used when the subject of the infinitive is the same as the subject of the sentence.

- As a noun, it has case relations. The infinitive itself is not inflected, but its case may usually be observed by its function in the sentence or by the article and/or the preposition with which it is sometimes used.

In the N.T., the infinitive and *hina* (ινα) clauses are used interchangeably.

II. Uses of the Infinitive

A. Equivalent of an Adverbial Clause

1. Purpose

Mt. 2:2 We have come <u>to worship</u> Him, i.e., Mk. 1:24; I Cor. 1:17
- with εἰς: Mt. 26:2 The Son of Man is delivered <u>to be crucified</u>. (I Thess. 3:5)
- with πρός: Mt. 6:1 Do not your righteousness ("alms") <u>to be seen</u> of men. (Mt. 5:28; 13:30)
- with ὥστε: Mt. 27:1 The elders took counsel…<u>to put</u> Him to death. (Lk. 9:52)
- with τοῦ: Mt. 13:3 A sower went forth <u>to sow</u>. (Mt. 2:13; 24:45)

2. Result (easily confused with *purpose*)

Heb. 6:10 God is not unjust <u>to forget</u> your work.

- with ὥστε: Mt. 27:14 He answered not a word <u>so that the governor marveled</u> (Mk. 1:27; 2:1)
- with τοῦ: Rom. 7:3 She is free from the law <u>so that she would not be</u> an adulteress (Mt. 21:32)
- with εἰς: Gal. 3:17 The law cannot annul <u>so that the promise is</u> of no effect. (Acts 7:19; I Thess. 2:15)

3. Time
- Antecedent time with πρίν: Mt. 26:75 <u>Before the cock crows</u> twice. (Mk. 14:30)
    with πρό: Mt. 6:8 Your Father knows what ye have need of <u>before ye ask</u>. (Gal. 2:12; 3:23; Acts 23:15)
- Contemporaneous time with ἐν τo: Mt. 13:4 <u>As he was sowing</u>. (Mt. 13:24; Mk. 4:4; Lk. 1:21)
- Subsequent time with μετὰ τò: Mt. 26:32 <u>After I have risen</u>. (Mk. 1:14; 14:28)

4. Cause
- With διὰ τò: Mt. 13:5 Seed sprang up <u>because it had</u> no depth of earth. (Mk.4:5)

(uses of the infinitive continued)

   B. Equivalent of a Noun Clause

     1. Subject
       Mt. 3:15 It is fitting…<u>to fulfill all righteousness</u>. (Mk. 2:9; 6:18; 9:10)

     2. Direct Object or Complementary
       Mt. 1:19 He was not willing <u>to make</u> an example of her. (Mk. 1:34,40; 2:4; 4:1)

     3. Indirect discourse
       Mt. 18:25 The Lord commanded him <u>to be sold</u>. (Mt. 19:21, Mk. 1:34; 12:18)

     4. Apposition
       Jas. 1:27 Pure religion is this, <u>to visit</u>. (Acts 15:18; Rom. 4:13)

   C. Explanatory or Modifying

     1. Explaining a Noun
       Mt. 3:14 I have need <u>to be baptized</u> of Thee. (Mk. 2:10)

     2. Explaining an Adjective
       Mt. 3:11 I am not worthy <u>to take off</u> His sandals. (Acts 23:15; Rev. 4:11; Mk. 1:7)

     3. Explaining a Verb (epexegetical)
       Acts 15:10 Why tempt ye God <u>to put a yoke on</u> the disciples. (Mk. 6:31) (Sometimes with a mild purposeful force.)

   D. Imperative (very rare)

     This is an independent use. The infinitive is substituted for a finite verb. Phil. 3:16 As ye received, <u>by this walk</u> (Acts 23:26; Titus 2:2)

Greek Ready Reference #3:
The Participle in Koine Greek

I. General

The participle is a verbal adjective:
- as a verb, it has tense and voice, and may have a subject and/or an object.
- as an adjective, it is declined, and has gender and number. Like an adjective, it will be either attributive or predicate in its position and will <u>always</u> modify something.

The temporal significance of the participle is determined by its relationship to the main verb.

- the present participle generally expresses action contemporaneous to the main verb.
- the aorist participle generally expresses action antecedent to the main verb, but also is used for contemporaneous action.
- the perfect participle expresses action antecedent to the main verb.
- the future participle generally expresses action subsequent to that of the main verb.

II. Uses of the participle

A. Adjectival Participles (attributive position)- always have the article

   1. Pure adjective Mk. 1:38; Jn. 4:10-11 APN (<u>A</u>rticle-<u>P</u>articiple-<u>N</u>oun)

   2. Substantival (usually with the article) AP

      A substantival participle may occur in any case with any noun use. Mk. 1:3,32; 3:34; 4:3; 5:14; 6:2; Jn. 3:16; 7:50 Subst.-Appos.

   3. Restrictive Attributive (might be called apposition under #2) APAN or ANAP. Mk. 3:3,22; Jn. 5:2; 6:50.

   4. Ambiguous – no article.

      All articular participles are adjectival in use.
      All attributive participles may be translated with a relative clause.

B. Adverbial Participles (predicate position)- never have the article.

   1. Circumstantial

- Attendant of circumstance Mk. 1:5,18,25; 2:3; 3:5,11; Jn.12:36b
- Time (when-while-as-after) Mk.1:10,16,19; Jn. 9:35.
- Cause (sometimes with ὡς) Mk.5:33; 6:20; 7:3; Mt. 2:3,10; Eph. 2:4
- Manner (sometimes with ὡς) Mk. 1:4,14,22,39,40
- Condition (if) Gal. 6:9; I Tim. 4:14; Heb. 2:3

- Concession (though) Mk. 4:12,31; 6:26; 8:18; Jn. 12:37
- Means (by) Mk. 1:31; Mt. 6:27; Jn. 12:15
- Purpose (in order that) Mt. 27:49

2. Genitive Absolute (may express any of the above circumstantial uses) Mk. 1:32; 4:17,35; 5:2,18,21; 6:2,21-22

3. Complementary or supplementary

- Periphrastic (any form of εἰμί plus a participle to complete the verb

	Verb	Participle
Present Periphr.	present	& present ptcp. Mk. 5:41; Mt. 5:25; 27:33
Imperfect Periphr.	imperfect	& present ptcp. Mk. 1:6,13,22; 10:32; Jn. 3:23
Future Periphr.	future	& present ptcp. Mk. 13:25
Perfect Periphr.	present	& perfect ptcp. Jn. 2:17; 3:21; Eph. 2:8
Pluperfect Periphr.	imperfect	& perfect ptcp. Mk. 6:52; Jn. 3:24; 12:16
Future Perfect Per.	future	& perfect ptcp. Mt. 16:19; 18:18

- Completing a verb (sometimes a predicate adjective)
  It is hard to tell in some instances whether this use is attributive or predicate. Mk. 3:1; 8:17; 9:3; 11:10; Gal. 1:22; Rev. 1:18; Jn. 1:6

- Indirect discourse
  Mk. 1:10,16; 5:31,36; 6:33,48; 8:30; Jn. 1:29,32; 7:32

4. Imperative (equivalent to a finite verb) Mk. 5:23 cf, Mt. 9:18

C. Ambiguous- no article. The reader is left to decide if the participle is attributive or predicate, and then to locate it exactly.

Greek Ready Reference #4
Interpreting Conditional Sentences in the New Testament

A conditional clause is a statement of supposition (generally introduced in English by the conjunction "if") the fulfillment of which is assumed as necessary to the fulfillment of a potential fact expressed in a companion clause. Grammarians call the "if" clause the "protasis": the main or fulfillment clause is called the "apodosis". Perhaps an illustration will suffice:

(Protasis – condition)   (Apodosis – fulfillment)
"If Christ is my Savior, then I am going to heaven."

Four Classes of Conditional Sentences

In interpreting conditional sentences in the New Testament, the student of the English Bible must realize that four classes of conditional sentences are used. In other words, the writers of the New Testament had four ways of saying "if", each with its distinct construction, meaning and significance (actually 5 ways if one includes the adverbial participle of condition). There are no equivalents to these constructions in English, but in this discussion, we will attempt to give some clues and suggestions as to how to recognize and discern types of conditional sentences. For purpose of simplification, consider these four types of conditional statements:

Type 1   "If" and it is assumed to be true, then…(apodosis)
              Example – If he is studying (and I assume he is), he will learn Greek.

Type 2   "If" and it is assumed not true, then…(apodosis)
              Example – If he had studied (and I assume he did not), he would have learned Greek.

Type 3   "If" and it has not happened, but it probably will and when it does, then…(apodosis)
              Example – If he studies (and he has not but maybe he will), then he will learn Greek.

Type 4   "If" and it has not happened, and it probably will not, but if it does, then…(apodosis)
              Example – If he would study (and he has not and he probably will not), then he would learn Greek.

These are examples of the four types or classes of conditional sentences used in the New Testament.

We will further simplify by viewing the four types of conditional sentences this way:

Type 1   <u>Reality</u>: that is, this construction affirms or assumes the reality of the condition. The author or spokesperson assumes the condition to be true due to reality or for the sake of argument. The "if" in many cases could be translated "since".

See Rom. 6:5,7 where "if" would be best translated "since".
See Gal. 5:18; Rev. 20:15.

Type 2   <u>Unreality</u>: that is, this construction is contrary to fact condition. The protasis or "if" clause is assumed to be false by the writer or spokesperson.

See Luke 7:39 where the Pharisee's doubt is expressed by this second class construction making it clear that he had no faith at all, since the contrary to fact construction is used.

See how a proper knowledge of this construction strengthens Paul's argument in Gal. 1:10.

Type 3   <u>Probability</u>: the construction that indicates probable future condition. It expresses that which is not really taking place but which probably will take place in the future.

See Mt. 9:21 – Note the faith implied in this construction.
See also Rom. 7:2; Heb 6:3.

Type 4   <u>Desirability</u>: the construction expresses that which is not now a reality and has little prospect of becoming a reality, but it would be desirable to be reality.

I Pet. 3:4 is perhaps the clearest example of this in the N.T. where the idea is "But even <u>if you should</u> suffer for righteousness' sake, you would be happy".

In other words, you are not now suffering for righteousness' sake, and while it is possible, it is not probable that you will.

Of these four forms of conditions, the New Testament uses the first two with great frequency, the third quite often, but the fourth very rarely and never in full form.

More on Hebrews 6:4-6

Hebrews 6:4-6 and 10:26-31 are two of the most difficult and variously interpreted passages in this epistle.[1] The first is in a context of retrogression; the second in one that deals with the absolute finality and efficaciousness of the death of Christ.

Hebrews 6:4-12 and 10:26-29 Compared

A Comparison of these two paragraphs in most interesting.

- Both are somewhat hypothetical, yet virtual realities, as indicated by, "if" condition(s), 6:4 & 6a; 10:26 (see p. 73 on 6:6).

- Both contexts contain information intended to produce change in thinking and practice.

- Both speak of impending, potential judgment by God, 6:7-8; 10:28-36

- Both state an emphatic confidence by the author that indicates that the hypothetical scenario is a warning, a shock treatment, to snap them out of their lethargy, 6:9; 10:39.

A look at the actual statements makes the comparison more graphic.

The Charge, 6:4a&6

"It is impossible to renew <u>*again*</u> *to repentance…" certain ones "who fall away…" or "<u>if</u> falling away"*

The Charge, 10:26-27

"<u>If</u> we (emphatic: author includes himself) sin willfully[2] after we have received knowledge (epignosis) of the truth,[3] There remains no more sacrifice for sins…"

The Potential Judgment, 6:7,8

"The earth which…bears thorns and briers…is rejected and near to being cursed…" Its production will be burned.

The Potential Judgment, 10:27a-30b

"There remains…'a certain' fearful expectation of judgment…The Lord will judge His people."

---

[1] In general, there are three major understandings of these paragraphs. 1) Some say these teach that one can believe and then lose his salvation by apostatizing out of the faith. I have two favorite questions for persons of this view: "How can a born again person become unborn?" and, "How long is <u>eternal</u> life?" 2) Others say that these warnings are for unsaved people who have stopped short of true faith in Jesus Christ: that they were "almost" believers, professors but not possessors of eternal life. To these I ask, "Have you seriously studied the context and the people addressed in the warning sections of Hebrews?" They can only be believers. 3) The third view is that these passages are addressed to true believers to encourage them to go on in the faith. This is my view with one major qualification (as discussed in this paper): they were Jewish believers who were being pressured to return to Temple sacrifices.

[2] Gen absolute of condition, hence "<u>If</u> we…" Εκουσίως γὰρ <u>ἁμαρτανόντων ἡμῶν</u> …

[3] "the knowledge of <u>the</u> truth:" both nouns have the definite article. The truth here is the fact that "There remains no more sacrifice for sins" as stated in 10:18 & 26. There is no forgiveness for anyone who goes to the wrong source for forgiveness (such as Levitical sacrifices).

<table>
<tr><td valign="top" width="50%">

The Stated Reasons, 6:6b

"Since 1) they keep on crucifying to themselves the Song of God, and
2) keep on putting Him to open shame?"

Both 1 & 2 are present, active, adverbial participles of cause, hence the translation "since", or "seeing that"(KJV).

</td><td valign="top" width="50%">

The Stated Reasons, 10:29

"How much worse punishment (than those who died under Moses' law),
1) he who has trampled under foot the Son of God,
2) has regarded as common the blood of the covenant by which he was sanctified,
3) and has insulted the Spirit of grace."

</td></tr>
</table>

-Note: Both paragraphs describe a virtual reality stated hypothetically in which the Jewish believer stiff-arms the grace of God.

<table>
<tr><td valign="top" width="50%">

The Author's Confidence, 6:9

"But, Beloved, we are confident of better things concerning you, things that accompany salvation, though we speak in this manner."

</td><td valign="top" width="50%">

The Author's Confidence, 10:39

"But we are not of those who draw back to perdition, but of those who believe to the saving of the soul."

</td></tr>
</table>

Those Addressed in the Book of Hebrews

Without question, internal evidence and logic establish that the readers were GENUINE believers: not "ALMOST" believers. AND, MOST IMPORTANTLY, THEY WERE JEWISH BELIEVERS. Internal statements such as 3:1; 4:16; 5:12; 6:1,19; 10:24: 12:28; 13:20,21 could be made only of believers.[4] Logically: all scripture is for the believer: it serves as a basis for doctrine, conviction, correction, and instruction (2Tim. 3:16). Moreover, why write scripture to an unbeliever? Scripture is written about unbelievers, but not to unbelievers.

Though believers, they were somewhat unique for they were Hebrew Christians confronted with the ongoing ritual of the Jewish Temple and the confusing doctrines of first century Judaism. Under severe persecution (10: 32-33), they had suffered social, political, economic, and religious banishment in their ethnic communities, and worst of all, ostracism from their families.

Under these conditions, they were tempted to return to the Temple sacrificial system. In so doing, they would trample under foot the Son of God, regard His blood/death as common or unclean, and do despite to the Spirit of grace, 10:29. IN OTHER WORDS, THEY WERE TEMPTED TO RETURN TO THE SACRIFICIAL SYSTEM OF PERVERTED JUDAISM, A

---

[4] Only believers could be addressed and exhorted thusly: "holy <u>brethren</u>, partakers of the heavenly calling" 3:1; "let <u>us</u> come boldly to the throne of grace that <u>we</u> may obtain mercy & find grace" 4:16; "for when for the time <u>ye ought to be teachers</u>, ye have need that one teach you again which be the first principles of the oracles of God" 5:12; "let <u>us</u> go on to perfection" 6:1; "which hope <u>we</u> have as an anchor of the soul" 6:19; "having therefore, <u>brethren</u>, boldness to enter into the holiest by the blood of Jesus" 10:19; "let <u>us</u> consider one another to provoke unto love and good works" 10:24; "wherefore receiving a kingdom which cannot be moved, let <u>us</u> have grace, whereby <u>we</u> may serve God acceptably…" 12:28; "now the God of peace… <u>make you perfect</u> in every good work to do his will, working in you that which is well pleasing in his sight, through Jesus Christ" 13: 20 & 21.

FORM OF RETROGRESSION THAT IS IMPOSSIBLE TODAY! Both paragraphs, 6:4-6 and 10:26-31, are hypothetical situations that must be understood in the contexts in which they are found.

Regardless, seeking forgiveness of sin via the wrong source, in this case Levitical sacrifices, is futile. The blood/death of Messiah so efficiently and effectively cares for sin that there remains no more sacrifice for sin.

This entire book is characterized by teaching followed by parenthetical warnings with admonitions. The warnings are primarily for these Hebrew Christians encouraging them to go on in the faith, that is, for their faith to mature in Phase 2 Christianity. The author is not encouraging them to become Christians, rather to grow as Christians. The warning/admonition sections are as follows: 2:1-4; 3:7-4:13; 5:11-6:20; 10:26-39; 12:14-17; 12:25-29; 13:9. Hebrews 6:4-6 is part of the third parenthetical warning; 10:26-39 part of the fourth parenthetical warning.